D0862338

LAST YEAR, when things were a little dull around the office and we were waiting around in between important publication dates, this publishing house issued a little book called *Pogo*. Several of the important officials in the office didn't understand why, and didn't even understand the book when they saw it. So, rather nervously, the book's proponents prepared a little one-column advertisement, hesitantly plunked up the few dollars necessary to run it, and waited.

They waited approximately 24 hours. A joyful shriek arose from Pogo fans throughout the nation who had been irritably clipping and pasting up the individual strips. Before the frantic telegrams from booksellers had been cleared away more than 200,000 people had rushed into bookstores and borne their copies fondly home.

Well, here's the new book about Pogo. It's no bigger than the last one, it's the same size. It's no better, it's just about the same sort of stuff. It contains the reasons why several hundred thousand *I Go Pogo* buttons are already being worn on undergraduate lapels throughout the country. The people who don't understand Pogo are fewer in number now, and hoarser. If you are one of them, you have been wasting your time reading this blurb.

I GO POGO

WALT KELLY

DOVER PUBLICATIONS
GARDEN CITY, NEW YORK

Copyright

Bibliographical Note

This Dover edition, first published in 2019, is an unabridged republication of the work originally published by Simon and Schuster, Inc., New York, in 1952.

Library of Congress Cataloging-in-Publication Data

Names: Kelly, Walt, author, artist.
Title: I go Pogo / Walt Kelly.
Other titles: Pogo (Comic strip)
Description: Garden City, New York : Dover Publications 2019. | "This Dover edition, first published in 2019, is an unabridged republication of the work originally published by Simon and Schuster, Inc., New York, in 1952."
Identifiers: LCCN 2019018634 | ISBN 9780486838359 (print) | ISBN 0486838358 (print)
Subjects: LCSH: Comic books, strips, etc.
Classification: LCC PN6728.P57 K36 2019 | DDC 741.5/973—dc23
LC record available at https://lccn.loc.gov/2019018634

Manufactured in the United States of America
838358005 2022
www.doverpublications.com

"HOW PIERCEFUL GROWS THE HAZY YON!
HOW MYRTLE PETALED THOU!
FOR SPRING HATH SPRUNG THE
CYCLOTRON,
HOW HIGH BROWSE THOU, BROWN COW?"

CONTENTS

SLIGHTLY HOLIDAZED

BUN RABBIT! WHAT'S YOU SO FIRED UP 'BOUT?
IT'S A OUTRAGE! ALL THESE HOLIDAYS CLOG-HOPPIN' UP THE YEAR... I'M GONE MARCH ON WASHINGTON AN' DEE-MAND OUTRAGE ACTION!
THE HON. GEORGE BIGGERS
"PUT DOWN THAT PIANO!" I'M GONE SAY, "AN' FIX OUR HOLIDAY SITUATION!" .... EVERY TIME A MAN WANTS TO WORK, HE GOT A VACATION STARIN' HIM IN THE FACE.

BY THE WAY, HOW FAR IS IT TO WASHINGTON?
GOIN' RIGHT THRU TREES AN' PARKED CARS IT'D BE 'BOUT SIX HUNNERD MILE.

FOOSH! THEY SURE BUILT THAT CAPITOL AWFUL FAR UP THE CREEK ... FIGGER THEM FOLKS UP THERE GITS OUTEN TOUCH WITH US OL' MORTAL CRITTURS HERE AT THE HEAD WATERS?

HOW D'YOU PREEPOSE TO SAVE TIME ON THESE HOLIDAYS, BUN RABBIT?
FOR EXAMPLE... LOOKY AT YOU.... NOT CELEBRATIN' ANY HOLIDAY AT ALL, BUT ME, I'M BUSY BUSYBUSYBUSYBUSY..

BUSY?
RIGHT NOW I'M CELEBRATIN' ST. VALENTINE'S DAY! WOW! HEARTS AN' FLOWERS! YAY!

I'D HATE TO HEAR YOU ON FOURTH OF JULY...
WOWIE! VALENTINE'S DAY--'RAY!

VALENTINE'S DAY USUAL IS A TIME FOR SWEET SENTIMENT.
INSIDE I'M CRAWLIN' WITH TENDERMINTS BUT OUTSIDE ALL HOORAW!
THINK THIS HOLIDAY MISHAP WILL MAKE MY DRUM SOGGY?

IF YOU IS GONE CELEBRATE ALL HOLIDAYS AT ONCE, DO YOU GOTTA TAG AFTER ME?
YEA!
YEA! ST. JOHN'S EVE!

I IS LOYAL, POGO... I STARTS WITH YOU, I FINISHES WITH YOU--- YEOWEE! WALPURGIS NIGHT RAH!
BE NICE DO HE START CELEBRATIN' MAW'S DAY, POGO.

MOTHER'S DAY! RAW! RAW! RAW!
RAW?
THAT ALL HE GONE DO? HE DIN'T EVEN PUT IN A PLUG FOR THE FLOWERS.
THAT'S IT... HE MORE PULLS PLUGS OUT THAN PUTS 'EM IN.
H'RAY! HODENING!
?

WHAT IN THE EVERLOVIN' BLUE EYED WORL' IS A-GOIN ON?
OL' BUN RAB IS CELEBRATIN' ALL HOLIDAYS AT ONCE.
THE NEW JERSEY BIG SEA DAY! RAH-RAH-RAH.. FARMER'S WASH DAY!
HE SAY HE'S DOIN' IT TO SAVE TIME AN' GIT 'EM OVER WITH...
DICK WATTS

THAT'S GONNA SKOOSH ALL THEM DAYS DOWN IN A LUMP AT ONE END OF THE YEAR LIKE TEETH PASTE.
YEAH... WHAT IS YO' GONE DO WITH THE REST OF THE YEAR AFTER IT'S ALL EMPTIED OUT?
ADMIRAL DICK WATTS
ARBITER ELEGANTIAE
UM... I'LL, UH, FILL IT UP WITH SATURDAY AFTER-NOONS AN' RENT IT TO THE NATIONAL LEAGUE... YEAY! HOLLE KREISH! LAA BOALDYN!
'RAH
RAH
WOW
WOW

HOORAY! I SAY, HOORAY FOR CROMM DUB'S SUNDAY!
STOP DRUMMIN UP HOLIDAYS 'TIL POGO'S HEAD-ACHE IS GONE.
OH, YOU GIT A HEADACHE FROM MY DRUMMIN? WELL, I GOT A NICE HOLIDAY WITH NO DRUMMIN'.
MM.. THEY DON'T MAKE ICE TASTY THESE DAYS.

GIT A LOAD OF THIS... NOT A LICK OF DRUMMIN' TO IT. TUAN YANG, THE DRAGON BOAT FESTIVAL.

BAM!
NICE, HUH? IT COMES ON THE FIFTH DAY OF THE FIFTH MOON AN'..
OH, THEM FIFTHS IS JES' FINE FOR CELEBRATIN'...

ALL THIS CELEBRATIN' YOU IS DONE IS GUV POGO A HEADACHE... ISN'T YOU 'BOUT OUT OF HOLIDAYS?
NOPE, THEY'S A WHOLE SLEW OF 'EM LEFT.

THERE'S HOGMANAY, THE CAKE DAY; THERE'S THE SOIRÉE OF GUMBO YA-YA .... ST. ELMO'S FIRE DRILL ---GOWK STORM DAY...

THE MIDWINTER BEAR SOCIETY DANCE; (HOLE UP SOME FINGERBONES) THE DOWN UNDER CORRO-BORREE; THE FESTA STULTORUM; THE DAY OF THE KA.

LAMMAS EVE; THE NIMAN KACHINA; UNCLE CHARLIE'S ANNUAL SHIVAREE; MARTINMAS; THE FEAST OF THE HUNGRY GHOSTS; KNIGHT RUPERT'S VISITING DAY.....
SAVE ONE FOR MY BIRTHDAY... I ALLUS GIVES THAT A REAL ROUSIN'.

I HEAR TELL YOU FELLAS IS CELEBRATIN' HOLIDAYS FER FOLKS.
WELL, IN A WAY, YES... RIGHT NOW BUN RABBIT IS CELEBRATIN' THE TAR OUTEN ABBOT'S BROMLEY ANTLER DANCE.

FIGGER HE'D HAVE TIME TO OBSERVE IGOR'S DAY WITH A LI'L' DIGNIFIED SCREAMIN' AN' DRUMMIN'?

IGOR'S DAY? NEVER HEERD OF IT ---WE GOT ALL WE CAN HANDLE WITH REGULATION SOUTHERN BONA FRIED HOLIDAYS LIKE THE FEAST OF GOIBNIU!
WELL! LET'S GO, UNCLE IGOR! STUFFY IS AS STUFFY DO!
WHAT'S UNTIED? WHITSUNTIDE? WHAT'S UNTIED ON WHITSUNTIDE? RAH!

HERE I IS! HERE I IS IS-IS-IS! I HURRIED OVER SOON AS I HEARD.
YOU MUST OF IS HEERD SOME-THIN' WE ISN'T GUY EAR TO.
WHY, YOU IS IN THE BUSINESS OF CELE-BRATIN' HOLIDAYS. SO I THUNK OF ONE AN' RUSHED OVER.
WHAT IS IT?

THIS IS THE DAY THE PEACE TREATY BETWEEN THE U.S. AND A. AND ENGLAND WAS RATIFIED.
DECLARED PEACE ON 'EM, HUH? MAN, I DIN'T EVEN KNOW WE'S MAD AT THE RASCALS.
WELL, ACTUAL IT WAS 'BOUT 167 YEARS BACK.
THEM PEACE THINGS IS FRAGILE--- US COULD WAIT A BIT AN' SEE IS THIS'N PERMAMINT!

JUST THOUGHT OF A REAL ROUSER TO CELEBRATE --- TODAY IS WHEN WE DISCOVERS THE HAWAIIAN ISLAN'S.
WE DID?
GOO-OOD FER US!
OR WAS IT NEXT WEEK OR MEBBE THIRDSDAY?
HEY, FLEAS! DID US DISCOVER HAWAII THIS WEEK OR LAS'?
HUMPH!

AS I WAS SAYIN', FERD, AFORE US IS SO RUDIMENTLY INNERUMPTED.... GITTIN' MARRIED IS BUYIN' A PIG 'N A POKE.
WELL, MERT, MY MARRYIN' UNCLE SAY HE GOT ALL PIG...
AN' NO POKE... NOT SO MUCH AS A NICKEL.
SHE DIN'T HAVE NO SCRATCH, HUH?
THEM FLEAS IS ALLUS TALKIN' SHOP.

WE'RE CELEBRATIN' HOLIDAYS AN' RABBIT THUNK UP A JOKE 'BOUT 'EM --- HE SAY: "D'YOU KNOW OUR FIRST HOLIDAY IS THE FOURTH?"
HAW?
THOSE CELEBRANTS TOLD A REAL MERRY ONE ---- SEEMS TWO GENTLEMEN ARE IN A HOLIDAY MOOD AN' ONE, WITH A SLY CHUCKLE, SAYS: " DO YOU REALIZE
U.S.

THAT WE AMERICANS HAVE A RARITY? OUR FIRST HOLIDAY IS INDEPENDENCE DAY?!?" GET IT, SIR? OUR A.NO.1 HOLIDAY FALLS ON THE FOURTH OF JOO-LY...
HO? HA? HEE?
US
NEVER MIND LEAVIN' MAIL FROM NOW ON --- I AIN'T TAKIN' OFF YOU NO MORE!

'CORDIN' TO MY POCKET CALENDAR, THIS IS THE ANNIVERSITY OF THE DISCOVERMINT OF THE PACIFIC OCEAN.
HOW COME? THIS MONTH AIN'T SEPTEMBER.
LOOK! IT SAY RIGHT HERE ON THE CALENDAR: SEPT -- TEE --- EM --- BEE -- ARE ...
PHOO. THIS HERE'S MO' LIKE JANUARY.

BUT IT MUST BE SEPTEMBER --- FOLKS BEEN USIN' THAT OCEAN FOR QUITE A SPELL --- COULDN'T DO THAT WITHOUT IT'S DISCOVERED.
MR. BALBOA IS DID IT ----- COUPLE YEAR BACK -- BOY FROM OVER SPAIN WAY.
ANYWAYS, THEY ISN'T NO JANUARY ON MY POCKET CALENDAR -- SO!
COMIN' DOWN TO IT, YOU ISN'T GOT ANY POCKET, EITHER.

POGO, I CLAIMS IT'S SEPTEMBER AN' POOR CHURCHY SAY IT'S JANUARY ---- TELL HIM WHICH ... STRAIGHTEN HIM OUT!
JES' A MINUTE, I'LL LOOK.
MM ...

SHUCKS! SHE'S STOPPED.
MUST BE JANUARY--- SHE ALLUS FREEZES UP IN WINTER --- IN SEPTEMBER SHE RUNS SLICK AS A WEASEL. TWO HOURS TO THE DAY.... FASTEST RUNNIN' CLOCK IN WARE COUNTY.
CIRCLE-STANTIAL EVIDENCE.
ANYWAY, A MORAL VICTORY FOR LOVABLE ME.

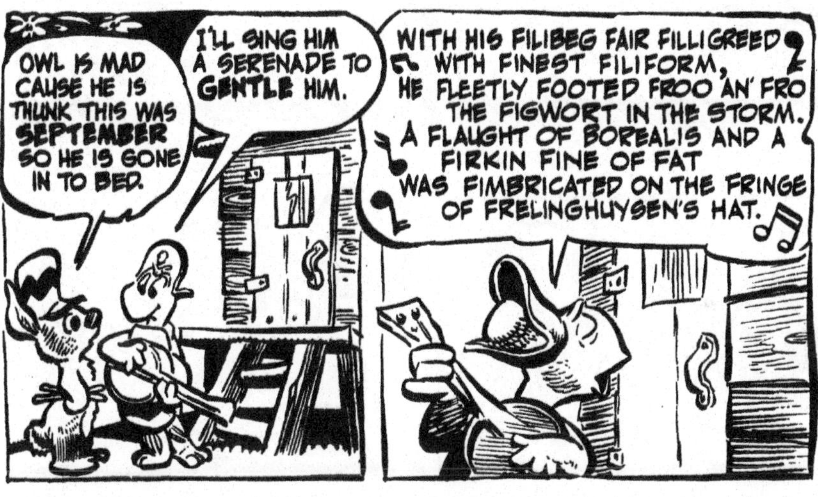
OWL IS MAD CAUSE HE IS THUNK THIS WAS SEPTEMBER SO HE IS GONE IN TO BED.
I'LL SING HIM A SERENADE TO GENTLE HIM.
WITH HIS FILIBEG FAIR FILLIGREED WITH FINEST FILIFORM, HE FLEETLY FOOTED FROO AN' FRO THE FIGWORT IN THE STORM. A FLAUGHT OF BOREALIS AND A FIRKIN FINE OF FAT WAS FIMBRICATED ON THE FRINGE OF FRELINGHUYSEN'S HAT.

IS YOU SINGIN' IN PATAGONIAN OR MONOGOHELIAN?
IN ENGLISH! IN ONE HUNNERD PER CENT AMERICAN RED, WHITE AN' BLUE BLOODED ENGLISH! WHEN YOU GO TO SLEEP AN' WAKES UP, DOES YOU FERGIT EVER'THING?

I HEAR YOU AND TURTLE IS HAD A FIGHT 'BOUT THE DATE?
WELL, I IS HURT POOR OL' CHURCHY'S FEELIN'S... I OWES HIM A APOLOGY.
COME TO THINK OF IT, I HAD A DREAM 'BOUT MY PAL AN' ME--- SEEMS I DIED! GULP
AN' HE HEERD OF IT BUT HE WERE SO MAD AT ME, HE REFUSE TO A-TTEND MY LAST RITES...
THERE... THERE.

THERE I LAY IN THE COFFIN, COLD AN' BEAUTIFUL--- WAITIN' AN' WAITIN AN' WAITIN' AN'..
HE WAS MEBBE SICK.
HE WAS SICK? I WAS DEAD.
BY JING! CHURCHY, IF YOU WON'T GO TO MY FUNERAL, I WON'T GO TO YOURS!

THIS IS TOO THE MONTH OF JANUARY, YOU IGNOROMNIBUS!
A FIGHTIN' WORD! A FIGHTIN' WORD!
IGNOROMNIBUS! IGNOROMNIBUS! IGNOROMNIBUS! IGNOROMNIBUS!
HAW! THAT AIN'T THE WORD. GUESS AGAIN!

JANUARY THEN.... I SAYS: JAN-YOU-WARY!
STILL YOU DIN'T USE THE FIGHTIN' WORD! IS YOU FEARED TO GUV IT TONGUE A-GAIN?
WHUT OTHER WORDS DID I USE---LET'S SEE: "THIS... IS---TOO..."
IN CASE HE DARES REPEAT IT, POGO, PLEASE CONTROL YOUR TEMPER! DON'T START NOTHIN'.
HUH?

I CAN'T THINK OF THE WORD WHAT INSULTED YOU.
A GOOD THING! POGO IS RAGIN' TO DEE-FEND ME.
I IS?
LEMME SHOW YOU HOW IT WORK... SPOSE A BOY GOT A CHIP ON HIS SHOUL-DER...(HOLE IT UP A MINUTE, POGO.)

NOW, SPOSE A-NOTHER BOY KNOCK IT OFF... THEN, HE GOTTA COME TO MORTAL GRIP WITH...OOOP!
A-CHOO!
SEE THAT? HE DEE-LIBERATE KNOCKS IT OFF. YOU GONE STAND FOR THAT?
ALL I DIN WAS SNEEZE A LI'L' BITTY.

'LONG AS YOU WANTS ME AN' TURTLE TO FIGHT... WHAT DOES YOU WANT US TO FIGHT 'BOUT?
WHY HE COMED 'ROUND WITH A CHIP ON HIS SHOULDER, CLAIMIN' THIS WAS THE MONTH OF JANUARY...
HA
CAUSIN' DISSENSION... UPSETTING THE APPLE TREE! STICKING HIS FINGER INTO THE DIKE....
GOT HIM!

BICKERING AND BRANGLING! REBELL-ICOSELY PETTI-FOGGING!
GEE, I'M SORRY! WULL, OKAY.

GARBAGIN' UMBRAGE!
WHAT HE SAY?
HE BEG OFF ---- HE SAY HE GOTTA GO TO HIS GRAN'MAMMA'S FUNERAL.

TURTLE IS A TROUBLE MAKER!

MY, THAT'S REALLY LOUD, ISN'T IT?
OH, YES! LOVELY AN' LOUD---OWL IS JES' FINE AT HOOTIN' AN' HOLLOWIN'.

SOMETHIN' IS HAPPEN'.
HE IS MERE SCREECHED HIS VOICE OFF.
NOW I GOT A CHANCE, I BEEN TRYIN' TO TELL YOU: THEY ISN'T NO FISH IN THAT THERE CAN.
WELL, I ISN'T GOT NO BAIT WORKIN' EITHER---THAT WORM NEVER COME BACK FROM HIS GRAN'MAM'S FUNERAL.

WHAT AILS HIM?
HE HOLLERED SO LOUD HE IS BLOWED OUT HIS TALKIN' TUBES.
MEBBE HE IS JES' RUN DOWN---PARM ME WHILE I LISTEN AN' SEE IS HE TICKIN'!

A GOOD SHAKIN' WILL DO HIM GOOOD
HIC HIC HIC HIC HIC!
I GOT HIM GOIN'---HE MUS' OF IS JUS' HAD HIS MAINSPRING WRUNG UP TOO TIGHT.
BUT HE GOT HINK-UPS.
WELL, IT'S MORE THAN HE SAID IN TWO DAYS.

NO RHYME FOR REASON

YOU SAY THIS WORM GOT THE HEART OF A **POET**?
YEP... YOU GOTTA ADMIT HE'S A LONG FELLER.
LAST YEAR I WROTE "*OWED TO A GRECIAN EARN*", AND "*FIRE WHEN THE GRIDDLE'S READY.*"
THAT WAS ***GRIDLEY***, WASN'T IT?

IT CERTAINLY WAS --- *VERY GRIDDLE-Y*.... WE THOUGHT OF CALLING IT "A CHILE'S GUARDIN' OF VERSUS."
OR "*HOMINY GRITS IN A CORN POME?*"
IS YOU WROT ANY-THING LATELY?
WELL, I WROTE A LI'L' THING CALLED "***THE RUBAIYAT***" BUT SOME **A**-RAB SWIPED THE TITLE AFORE MY PUBLISHERS GOT GOIN'.
BY JONGO! IS *NOTHIN'* SACRED?
NOTHIN'!

I SPOSE A EDUCATED LI'L' SPRAT LIKE **YOU** IS A ***BOOK*** WORM?
NO, **I** IS A PLAIN ***ANGLE SPECIE***.
BAIT TYPE?
WATCH YO' LANGRIDGE! HUMBLE THO' I IS, I GOT A FIERCE ***PRIDE*** AND A ***PREJUDICE*** TO BOOT!
I WAS ***ONLY*** TRYIN' TO BE ***FRIENDLY***.

SO YOU IS WRITIN' A POEM?
YEP--- I IS LOOKIN' FOR A RHYME FOR PERPENDICULAR.
HOW 'BOUT "JUNE"?
JUNE?!
JUNE DON'T RHYME WITH PERPENDICULAR AND IT GOT NOTHIN' TO DO WITH MY POEM.
THEN START OVER AND WORK IT IN ----- FORGET PURPLE-DINCULAR. OOHH... YOU'LL THANK ME SOME SWEET DAY.

LISTEN, ALBERT, AT THE POEM THAT THE LI'L' WORM CRITTUR WROTE OUT OF HIS OWN SPECIAL BRAIN.
BAYOU LEAV'

OH, PRETTILY PREEN THE PRIMLY PROSE THAT BLOOMS AMIDST THE SNUNDAY SNOWS AND GLOOM THE GLIBLY GLEAMING GLOWS WHILE SUBTLY SUPPING SWEET SUPPOSE.

BY JING! I COULD WRITE A BETTER POEM THAN THAT WITH BOTH HEADS TIED BEHIND OF MY BACK.
PHOO! YOU MISSED ITS FRUITY IMPORT.
PHOO YO' OWN SELF... IT DON'T MEAN NOTHIN' AN' I DON'T UNNERSTAN' IT.!
YOU DON'T UNDERSTAN' RUSSIAN, SO RUSSIAN MEANS NOTHIN'?
NYET!
SPOKE LIKE A WHITE PRAVDA.

HOW CAN YO' MATCH WITS WITH A WORM WHAT GOT 45 DEGREES FROM PADUCAH U., GLASGOW AND THE SANTA FE R.R.?
BEIN' A HUMAN BEAN TYPE OF ALLIGATOR, I IS GOT 98.6 DEGREES FROM FAHREN-HEIT.
HAW! ALBERT CAN'T SPELL HIS WAY THRU A BOOK OF CIGARET PAPERS.
I BET I COULD!

WELL, YO' WILL HAVE TO HAVE A POETRY CONTEST.
A-GREED!
FUDDLE-STUCKS! I'LL OUTSCAN THAT LI'L' GRUB TWO TO ONE.
WELL! I'LL GO HOME AN' WORK ON MY I-AMBIC PENTAMETER.
BY TUNKIT, IF YOU USES ANY MACHINERY I'LL DECLARE A FOUL!

SO---YOU IS GOT YOURSELF INTO A POETRY CONTEST WITH A WORM.
YEP! AN' YOU GOTTA BE MY SECOND.
THE BAYOU LEAF
YO' SECOND? WHAT I MUST GOTTA DO?
WHEN I WRITES THE FIRST LINE, YOU WRITES THE SECOND.

I IS GONE AN' GOT MYSELF INTO A BATTLE OF WITS WRITIN' POETRY AGAINST A WORM AN' NOW I IS STUCK ON A TECHNICALORIE.
SUCH IS LIFE.

WHEN I WRITES IT'S HARD TO READ AT THE SAME TIME--- WHEN I READS I CAN'T SPELL SO GOOD AND WHEN I SPELLS GOOD I FERGETS HOW TO WRITE---
YOU GO 'HEAD AN' DICTATE---I'LL TAKE IT DOWN

"THE COCK DOTH CRAW, THE DAY DOTH DAW, THE CHANNERIN' WORM DOTH CHIDE. GIN WE BE MIST OUT O' OUR PLACE---- AN' SAIR PAIN WE MAUN BIDE."
HOLD ON!

IF YOU MADE THAT UP-- WHAT DOES IT MEAN?
MEAN? I MADE IT UP- I MADE IT RHYME- NOW I GOTTA MAKE IT MEAN SOMETHIN'!?

WELL, WHAT WAS YOU GONE CALL IT?
DER MOND IST AUFGEGANGEN

WHAT'S THAT MEAN?
JUST WHAT IT SAYS! DER MOND IST AUFGEGANGEN!

BUT WHAT DO IT MEAN? IT'S NOT ENGLISH!
AAH! YOU SPOILS EVERYTHING! I KNEW WHAT IT MEANT WHEN I THOUGHT IT WAS ENGLISH BUT NOW--- HOW DO I KNOW WHAT IT MEANS?

THIS POEM YOU WROTE, ALBERT--- THE METER KEEPS FALLIN' OFF--
WELL, LEAVE IT OFF -- IT AIN'T A TAXICAB.

YOU NEED IT! IT BREAKS DOWN INTO SO MANY FEETS PER LINE! THE WAY YOU GOT IT, THERE'S TOO MUCH OF A TAX ON THE PHONETICS.
SO, THE TAX PEOPLE IS PUTTIN' A METER ON MY POEM, HUH?

BY JING, I IS GONNA SECEDE! THE COST OF RUNNIN' THE GUMMINT IS---
AN' ANOTHER THING--- YO' SYNTAX IS ---

DON'T TELL ME! AS A SECRETARY, YOU IS MORE A TAX EXPERT, BUT BEFO' YOU TURNS IN YO' VISOR, REMEMBER, I IS A CLEAN LIVIN' AMERICAN ALLIGATOR

HOUN' DOG, I NEEDS A SECRETARY TO WRITE DOWN MY POEMS FOR THE BIG CONTEST-- KIN YOU WRITE?
TOLERABOBBLE

IF I DICTATES THESE POEMS TO YOU AN' YOU WRITES 'EM DOWN YOU'LL READ 'EM ---- YOU'LL KNOW WHAT'S IN 'EM! HOW CAN I BE SURE YOU WON'T SWIPE 'EM?

YOU'LL BE PERFECTLY SAFE, SIR --- I'LL TAKE DOWN YOUR POEMS IN SHORTHAND! I CAN'T READ SHORT HAND!
PERFECK!

THIS RHYMIN' DICTIONARY WHAT PORKYPINE LOANED ME THE BORRY OF IS SORTA PECULI·OUR.
MM?

LISTEN TO THIS FOR EGG-SAMPLE : RAT, CAT, BAT, SAT, FAT, CHAT, HAT, MAT
SOUNDS MIGHTY FOREIGN TO ME.
RHYMING DICTIONARY
RHYMING DICTIONARY

HOT DOG! YOU MEANS I IS BEEN READIN' A FOREIGN TONGUE?
MM--NO--WAIT!

THEY IS MERE PRINTED THE BOOK UPSIDE DOWN! HOW IS SHE NOW?
RHYMING DICTIONARY
NOT MUCH BETTER.

IF YOU WANTS TO REALLY WIN THE HEARTS OF THE JUDGES IN THIS POEM CONTEST, YOU'LL WRITE SOMETHING WITH A NOBLE SENTIMENT.

A THING OF STERLING IMPORT LIKE: Old Dog Tray's ever faithful --- Grief cannot drive him a-way --- He is gentle -- He is kind - You'll never, never find -
GULP

A truer friend --GULP AWK --HOOP-- A truer-SNFF-friend --BAW-HOO-HOO--- than Old-BRAHAHOO-Dog Tray.

DIDN'T THAT BREAK YOUR NATURAL BORN HEART?
ALL YOU IS BROKE IS MY SEE-GAR AN' YOUR CONTRACK.

MEBBE WHAT YOU NEEDS IS A GHOST WRITER FOR THIS POEM CONTEST.
SPSST!

WHO THAT WHAT GO SPSST?
ME ---SEMINOLE SAM! --- IT JUS' SO HAPPEN I IS GOT A GOOD GHOST WRITER, CHEAP.

THAT'S JES' DANDY.
KINDLY STEP THIS WAY...

HOWDY, FRIENDS ---- DR. SAM TELLS ME YOU'D LIKE A LITTLE GHOST WRITING DONE FOR A REASONABLE FEE.
R.I.P.

IF I GOTTA HAVE A WRITER, COULDNINT IT BE A LIVE ONE?
WHAT?! FLY IN THE FACE OF FASHION? GHOST WRITERS IS ALL THE RAGE.
DOES YOU USE NOTHIN' BUT TOMBSTONES TO WRITE ON?
A DISGUSTIN' HABIT.
AS A GHOST, SUPERNATURALLY NOTHIN' BUT.

I CERT'LY DO ADMIRE YOU PERFESSIONALS! HOW DOES YOU EVER REMEMBER HOW TO SPELL UNDER THERE IN THE DARK?
FOR THAT HE IS GOT ME, A GHOST SPELLER WHAT GITS HALF THE FEE.
WHAT?!

BLANKER VERSE WAS NE'ER BLUNK!

SO YOU IS THE WORM WHAT IS IN THE BIG POETRY CONTEST 'GINST ALBERT--- WHAT IS YOU THUNK UP SO FAR?

BLANK VERSE?
EXACTLY---- MY NEPHEW HERE CAN TRANSLATE

"THE WINTER WIND WINDS WANLY--"
TURN AROUND! TURN A-ROUND!

EXCUSE ME! "THE WINTER WIND WINDS WANLY--"
TRUTHFULLY, I THOUGHT IT HAD MORE TO IT THE OTHER WAY 'ROUND
HE'S YOUNG - SOMETIMES DOESN'T KNOW WHICH END IS NORTH

HEY! ALBERT IS HIRED A GHOST WRITER!

A REAL GENUINE LIVE GHOST WRITER?
YEP... HE'S CHIPPIN' OUT BLANK VERSE ON A TOMBSTONE FOR ALBERT.

A CALAMITY! A CALAMITY! THE RHYMIN' WORM WHAT'S IN THE CONTEST CRAWLED INTO MY BAIT CAN TO VISIT AN' NOW I CAN'T TELL WHICH IS WHACH.
I'LL FIX THAT.

WHICH OF YOU IS THE RHYMIN' WORM? 'CAUSE HE DON'T QUALIFY FER BAIT.
ME!
ME!
ME!
ME!
ME!
ME, TOO!

ALL THESE WORMS CLAIMS THEY IS THE RHYMIN' WORM.
SOMEBODY SHOULD GIVE 'EM A TEST.
THE VERY REASON I IS BRUNG OVER MY BAGPIPES.
YOU THERE, SIRRAH, STAND FORTH AN' RECITE A BIT OF VERSE TO THE MUSIC I PLAY.

ANYONE WHAT CAN'T DO IT IS NATURAL NOT THE RHYMIN' WORM.
GREAT, PORKY... JES' GREAT!
SKEE-WHEEK
KREEKEOW
SNEE-YOWR
ANY OF 'EM STAND FORTH?
THEY ALL STOOD FORTH AN' HIGH-TAILED IT FOR WORM COUNTRY.

WHEN YOU BLOWED THE PIPES BEFORE AN' SCARED AWAY THE RHYMIN' WORM, YOU ALSO SCARED CHURCHY'S HEAD-BONE BACK INTO HIS SHELL.
TELL HIM TO COME OUT, IT'S SAFE.
IT'S SO LONG SINCE HIS HEAD BEEN IN THE SHELL HE CAN'T GIT IT ON OUT.
EVERY TRADE HAS ITS HAZARDS.

HE SHUNTNA TOOK UP TURTLIN' IF HE CAN'T HANDLE THE JOB.
SHOOSH... HE'S SENDIN' OUT A MESSAGE.
WHAT'S THE WORD?
HE SAYS HE'S GLAD HE LEFT HIS HAT OFF 'CAUSE HE'S TOO POLITE TO WEAR IT INDOORS ---ALSO HOW 'BOUT SENDIN' IN A LI'L LUNCH?

LONG AS YO' HEAD BONE IS STUCK INSIDE THERE, CHURCHY, US OUGHTA HIRE SOMEBODY SMALL TO SIT ON TOP AN' STEER YOU.

WELL, SAY! JUS' WHO WE IS LOOKIN' FOR---- YOU WANT A JOB AS CHURCHY'S PILOT?
YEP, I JUS' LEFT A JOB DOIN' GHOST SPELLIN' FOR ALBERT'S GHOST WRITER IN THE POEM CONTEST.

THEY FIRED ME FOR SPELLIN' CABBAGE WITH ONLY ONE "W".
YOU'D BETTER WEAR THE HAT.
GUESS US COULD GO SEE HOW OL' ALBERT IS DOIN' .... COME ON.
OOP! HARD LEFT RUDDER! YOU ISN'T EVEN ON THE RUNWAY.
HMM! OL' TURTLE MUST OF HAS GONE GOTTEN A HAIRCUT.

STEER OL' CHURCHY OVER HERE, BUG..... 'LONG AS YOU IS HIS SEEIN' EYE HEAD WHILST HIS PERSONAL SKULL IS STUCK INSIDE HIS SHELL.
AHOY THE ENGINE ROOM! VEER TWO POINTS OFF YOUR STARB'D BROW.
HERE IS A POEM I IS WROT AS YO' GHOST WRITER, ALBERT, WHAT GOT A UNEARTHLY QUALITY ON HER.
"I love squash pie an' squishy slugs; What I loves best is skooshin' bugs."
HEY! HE DIN'T MEAN NOTHIN' PERSONABOBBLE!
HALP!
THE POEM IS SO GOOD, TURTLE LOST HIS HEAD OVER IT.
OH, I WRITES 'EM POWERFUL.

THE RHYMIN' WORM IS BACK AN' RARIN' TO START THE POETRY CONTEST.
OL' TURTLE WAS GONE BE JUDGE BUT HE'S SORTA OUTTA-SHAPE.

IT SEEM FUNNY TO HAVE A POETRY CONTEST JUDGE WHAT CAN'T SEE NOR CAN'T HEAR!

DIN'T YOU NEVER SEE THAT OL' STATUE OF JUSTICE? SO DON'T POKE FUN AT TURTLE HAVIN' HIS HEAD STUCK... HIS INFIRMARY AIN'T PERMANENT.

BESIDES YOU DON'T GOTTA SEE OR HEAR POETRY.....YOU MUST GOTTA FEEL IT.'
AN' THAT'S WHY I IS SANDPAPERED MY FEETS DOWN.
YOU IS GONE FEEL THE POEMS FOR HIM?
YEP, I IS SO SENSITIVE NOW I COULD STRADDLE THE CHATTAHOOCHIE BLINDY-FOLDERED AN' TELL BY MY FOOTS WHICH WAS GA., AN' WHICH WAS ALABAM.

IF YOU TWO IS READY FOR THE POETRY CONTEST, THE POETRY CONTEST IS READY FOR YOU.
OKAY... I IS ALL SET TO WIN.
SO AM I.
BAM!
THEN GO!

The meanin' of the Mornin', 'Midst the moanin' of the Moon, Bespeaks a specious speck of speech That quarters past the Noon.
UM-UH-UG UNK-WUMS. MM WP?
THE WORM WON THE SPRINT EVENT... LET'S PREPARE FOR A HEAT OF HURDLES, CHAPS.
FOUL! WE'RE S'POSED TO USE OUR OWN LANGUAGE.
THAT WAS MY OWN LANGUAGE ... MY VERY OWN.

READY FOR THE HURDLES IN THE POETRY CONTEST! GO!
BANG
I PROTEST! THE JUDGE NEVER HEERD MY LAST POEM.
THE JUDGE GOT HIS HEAD STUCK IN HIS SHELL AN' CAN'T HEAR NOTHIN' SO YOU CAN USE THE SAME POEM OVER.
BUT...

BUT..
The best of the worst is full alive; Tho' wurst is not at first --
No livery may deliver ME An aliver liverwurst.
THE WORM WINS THE HURDLES, TOO --- ANY QUESTIONS?
YEH.... WHAT'S HE TALKIN' 'BOUT?
THEM LI'L' SKINFLINKS IS CHEATIN' IN THIS POETRY CONTEST ----SO HOW 'BOUT YOU TAKIN' A NOTE INTO THE JUDGE FOR ME, HOP FROG?
I IS APPEALIN' TO THE JUDGE --- YOU IS BEATIN' THE GUN EVERY TIME WE BEGINS A NEW POEM --- I WANT A CLEAN START ---
I IS EVEN MORE APPEALIN' TO THE JUDGE AN' I SENT IN A NOTE, TOO.
GUB? WUMP? BZZZ - MMG ZOOP
CHURCHY SAY IT'S TOO DARK INSIDE TO READ ANYTHING 'CEPT MONEY OR A MENU ----
OH, FOOT!
WELL, BACK TO THE STARTIN' LINE... IF HE DIN'T READ MY NOTE, HE DIN'T READ YOURS EITHER.
WASN'T MUCH ON MY NOTE 'CEPT "FIVE DOLLARS" PRINTED IN EACH CORNER.

FELLOWS, I HAVE A PERFECTLY SPLENDID IDEA --- INASMUCH AS TURTLE'S HEAD IS STUCK HE CANNOT BE THE POETRY JUDGE.
WELL, WHAT'S SO SPLENDID 'BOUT THAT?
I DON'T MINE BEIN' CHURCHY'S EYE BUT I IS TIRED OF EATIN' HIS POP CORN FOR HIM, TOO.
BRACE UP... ONLY ONE BAG TO GO.
I'M WILLING TO BE THE POETRY JUDGE MYSELF.... CHEAP...
HOW CHEAP?
WELL... I'D DO IT FREE.
BUT WOULD YOU DO IT GOOD?
POGO, HOW CAN YOU LOOK A GIFT HORSE IN THE EYE?
WELL, NO SENSE WASTIN' HIGH CLASS JUDGIN' ON THE POETRY WHAT'S IN THE CONTEST, ANYWAY.
AS OLD TURTLE'S SEEIN' EYE, I IS MIGHTY TIRED OF HAFFIN' TO EAT HIS POP CORNS FOR HIM.
BUT HE LOVE IT SO!
BEIN' SUBSTITUTE JUDGE OF THE POETRY, I IS GONE APPLY PURE SCIENCE.
HOUN' DOG GOT A POETRY JUDGIN' MACHINE IN THE BAG WHAT APPLAUDS THE BEST STUFF... FAIR AN' SQUARE.
GREAT! A MACHINE TO LISTEN AND APPLAUD! WE CAN GO HOME.

NOW, THE POEM WHAT GITS APPLAUDED WINS.. WHAT'S THE TITLE OF YOURS, WORM?
MAN'S BEST FRIEND, THE NOBLE DOG!
CLAP!
CLAP! CLAP! CLAP! CLAP CLAP CLAP CLAP CLAP CLAP CLAP CLAP CLAP
MY SAKES! LOOKY WHAT WAS IN THE BAG! HEH--HEH-
NOT SO MUCH IN THE BAG AS YOU FIGGERED. LET'S HAVE A RE COUNT, JUDGE.

YOU IS TURTLE'S ASSISTANT, SO YOU GOTTA EAT ALL HIS POPCORN FOR HIM ...
BUT.. BUT...
I DEMANDS WE USE OL' CHURCHY FOR A JUDGE ... OL' DOG DON'T WANT TO HEAR NOTHIN' 'CEPT POEMS 'BOUT DOGS.
A HIGH TONE SUBJECK.
6-6
YOU THINK YOU C'N JUDGE THE POETRY EVEN IF YO' HEAD IS STUCK, CHURCHY?
PRINKLE WUMS GOPPLES OOBERWIK

CHURCHY LA FEMME SAY THE POETRY WILL GOTTA BE WEIGHTY... OOP! WHAT'S THAT?!
WHEERP!
OL' HOP FROG WAS HELPIN' CHURCHY BY EATIN' HIS POP CORN AN' HE FINALLY ET THE WHISTLE PRIZE .... IT GUV HIM A BAD CASE OF WHISTLE-CUPS.
WELL, HE GOTTA STOP HICCUPPIN' DURIN' THE CONTEST.
WHEE-ROOOP!
WHEEK!
TWEEERP!

WHY, YOU BUMP-HEADED BULL BAT, ALBERT'S POEM IS BEST!
AN' I SAY YOU'RE A OL' PUDDIN' EARED OCTOPUSH! THE WORM IS BETTER.
I'LL PEEL THE PAINT OFF'N YOUR PORCH, YOU PEANUT-POLLED PTERODACTYL!
I'LL FRICASSEE THE FAT OUTEN YOUR BALL-HEADED BEAN ... YOU--
Tush!

Softly -- softly, my dear chaps --- be calm and settle your differences with kindness and ~~~

HEY! WHAT'D HE DO?
AAAAAH --- HE'S ONE OF THOSE TROUBLE-MAKIN' PACIFISTS!

ALBERT, MEBBE WE CAN BUST OUT AN' SETTLE THIS POEM CONTEST--- NOW, YOU IS GOT MERE ONE POEM, RIGHT?
YEP, THAT I IS.

AND OL' TURTLE, THE JUDGE, SAID HE THOUGHT THE BEST POETRY WOULD BE THE WEIGHTIEST, RIGHT?
YEP, THAT HE DOOD.

IN THAT CASE, I WINS! US MIGHT'S WELL ADMIT MY 142 PRE-TESTED POEMS WRIT ON 142 PIECES OF PAPER WILL OUTWEIGH YOUR ONE PUNY POEM.
WELL, HERE'S WHAT MINE IS WRIT ON ... OUTWEIGH THAT!

I CAN'T READ MY 142 POEMS 'CAUSE ALBERT FLANG THAT OL' TOMBSTONE DOWN ATOP OF 'EM .... I PROTEST ...
NATURAL, IF WE CAN'T GIT THE STONE OFF'N THEM POEMS, WORM, ALBERT WILL WIN BY DEFAULT.
WHOOSH! SUDDENLY THIS STONE IS PICKED UP A LI'L' WEIGHT... 'BOUT A TON.

ALBERT'S POEM ON THE STONE CAN'T WIN UNLESS SOMEBODY KNOWS WHAT IT MEANS.
FROM WHAT I KNOW 'BOUT POEMS, IT CAN'T LOSE IF NOBODY KNOWS WHAT IT MEANS.
"SI QUAERIS PENINSULAM AMOENAM, CIRCUMSPICE." .. Hm, mebbe it means "The best part is underground."
LOOKY HERE!

JUDGE SAY HE DON'T WANT NO UNDERGROUND SUBVERSIVE POEMS.
WIPS GRIMMIS GOBF WM?
HERE'S ONE OF MINE WHAT IS LEFT!
Wretched Richard, richened sweet, By the fingers of his feet, Toted tuppence with his toes, Nodding nimbly next his nose... The mist must myrtle on the way While minst...
HEY! YOU HEERD THE RULING IN THE LAST PANEL!

ALBERT, US MOUGHT AS WELL ADMIT YOU DIN'T WRITE NO POETRY WORTH READIN' -- SO US GOTTA AWARD THE PRIZE TO THE WORM.
OH, NO, YOU DON'T! MR. WORM IS BEEN SWIPIN' ALL OF LI'L' BERNICE ELEANOR'S HOME WORK IN THE ENGLISH CLASS!
LI'L' BERNICE ELEANOR IS RESPONSIBOBBLE FOR THEM POETRIES.
HAW! COULDN'T EVEN RHYME AGIN A CHILE!
AW, SHE BUN TO KIDNEYGARTEN.
WELL, THE PRIZE GOES TO BERNICE. WHAT HAPPENED TO THAT WRAPPED BOOK OF EDGAR A. GUEST'S POEMS?
WOWP! THAT WAS POEMS? IT WAS SO PERTY, I THUNK IT WERE A CAKE ......
ME AN' OWL ET IT!
ANY GOOD?
NEMMINE, BERNICE HONEY, US'LL GO HOME AN' HAVE A BIRTHDAY.

IT IS HARD TO KEEP A HEAD

POGO, WHY EÉS EET HOW THESE TOORTLE, CHURCHY, HAS HEES HEAD STUCK EEN HEES SHELL, EEŞ EET?
WELL, IT'S A CONDITION LEFT OVER FROM THE POETRY CONTEST.
SHE EES NOT CATCHING OR CONTAGION, EES HE?
NOT 'LESS YOU IS A JUDGE OF SOMETHIN' AN' GOT A SHELL TO CRAWL INTO.

SO LONG AS I HAVE THESE BRANCH OF FLOWAIR EEN THERE, DO M. LE CAPTAIN CHURCHY MIND EEF I WATER THESE BRANCH?
OOORG!
ALORS! I HAVE OFFEND MY DEAR CAPTAIN... NO?
AARG * KOFF!
SOUTHERN GENT'MINTS LIKES A LI'L' FLAVOR WITH THAT BRANCH WATER.

I PUTS A LI'L' PERISCOPE IN THERE SO'S OL' TURTLE KIN SEE.
STEEL, HE HAVE QUEER LOOK-- HE NEED SOME-SING, NO? LE CHAPEAU!

AH, M'SIEUR EES GORGING! MAGNIFIQUE! I APPLAUD! TRÉS BEAU! LA VIAND ROSE! LE BATON ROUGE! LE FROMAGE BLEU

NO! NO!
I AM--- HOW YOU SAY HEEM---I AM--- WHAT EES THESE--? I AM--- M-- ALORS I AM.... I AM....
GROWL
POCK!
---EEN-O-SEENT!
DON'T BLOW NONE MY WAY.

I IS BRUNG SOME OL' DOCTORIN' TOOLS OVER SO'S MEBBE US KIN BLAST CHURCHY'S HEAD LOOSE.
HIS HEAD IS LOOSE ENOUGH; IT JEST IS KINDA SEE-CLUDED.
COULDN'T FOTCH MY GLASSES ON ACCOUNTS I USES 'EM TO HOME TO PLUG UP A HOLEY WINDOW---- NOW WHERE'S THE STETHOSCOPE ---? AH, HERE IT IS.

H'LO, OPERATOR, GIMME THE GROCERY STORE; THERE'S FOUR OR FIVE OF US IN HERE THAT COULD USE A GOOD SQUARE MEAL AND....
SSHH--POGO, DON'T LET ON, BUT IT 'PEARS TO ME LIKE OL' CHURCHY IS OVER-RODE WITH MICE--- HUNGRY MICE!
I TOLE HIM AN' I TOLE HIM: "PUT A SCREEN UP THERE," I TOLE HIM, "YOU HEAR, NOW?" THAT'S WHAT I TOLE HIM...

Money braves art is a·leap in the deep
HOWLAND, IS YOU FIGGERIN' OUT A WAY TO PRY OL' CHURCHY'S HEAD OUTEN HIS SHELL?

YEP, WE'LL BORE A HOLE HERE, SEND IN A CREW WITH DYNAMITE AN..
HOL' ON! CHURCHY SAY "NOTHIN' DOIN'!"

WHAT ARE YOU? ONE OF THEM ANTI-VIVISECESSIONISTS?
WELL, IT'S HIS OWN PERSONAL HEAD.

THEN WE'LL GOTTA GRAFT A OUTSIDE HEAD ON.
GRAFT? HE SAY HE AIN'T GOIN' INTO POLITICS EVEN IF HE ISN'T GOT A HEAD.

DOCTAIR HOWL, I AM HEAR THAT YOU ARE DEECIDE TO PUT ANOTHAIR HEAD ON M'SIEUR LE CAPTAIN CHURCHY LA FEMME --- SO, I AM BREENG CONDY-DATE WHAT HE HAS EVER-SEENG!

HUMPH! HE'S GOT WHAT?
OBSAIRVE.. HE HAS HEAD... NO?
AN' IT'S 'BOUT GOOD AS NEW.

NEVER HARDLY USED IT 'CEPT TO HAVE A FEW HEADACHES WITH....
READY?
HEADACHES? I DON'T WANT NO HEAD AS GITS HEADACHES.
BOT-..
AAANH--- WE WUNTNA BEEN COM-PATABOBBLE.
MY MEDICAL OPINION IS HE'D LOOK BETTER IN PURPLE ANYHOWS.
ME, A BIRD BRAIN? FOOY.
WHO DO I KNOW WHO EES POORPLE

I HAVE THESE WONDERFULS CAREER FOR M'SIEUR FROG, BUT I MUS' PAINT HEEM PURPLE FIRST--- EET EES THE COLOR DEMANDED...
PAINT HIM ANY COLOR YOU WANT SO LONG AS HE GO TO WORK.
PURPLE
DOCTAIR HOWL EES GONE TO GRAFT AN OUTSIDE HEAD ON TURTLE ---- AAH--- THE COLOR COMBINATION EES BEAUTIFUL...

A SPLENDEED JOB FOR M'SIEUR FROG--TRAVELING! DIRECTING! THEENKING! DOCTAIR OWL WILL TAKE YOUR HEAD AN' SEW IT ONTO...
WHAT!?
NOT BAD!
BUT M'SIEUR FROG, YOU ARE SO BECOMING!
SHUCKS!
I AIN'T BECOMIN' NOBODY'S HEAD EXCEPT MY OWN.
NOW WHAT AM I GONNA DO WITH A PURPLE HUSBAND?

WONDER HOW US WILL EVER GIT OL' CHURCHY'S HEAD OUTEN HIS SHELL?
OOP! IS YOU REAL OR JEST PRETENDIN'?
PRETENDING? HA!! Preposterous! A POSITIVELY PRECIPITOUS and Peerless PRESUMPTION, My dear SIR!

AN INTELLIGENT and INTELLECTUAL Youth SUCH AS You ☆☆☆ Must meet the Matchless Master of the Magical and MYSTERIOUS, The PENULTIMATE P.T. BRIDGEPORT!!

MAN! HE SOUNDS GOOD ENUFF TO EAT! WHO IS HE?
REJOICE! ---NONE OTHER THAN ME!

I, young sir am a CIRCUS MAN! P.T. BRIDGEPORT, by name, Here in search of ☆☆ TALENT ☆☆
☆☆TALENT☆☆? OH, YOU MEANS "TALENT."
YES, OUR OLD TROUPE, A FLEA CONTINGENT, got OUT of HAND !!!! and now we're Scratching the BOTTOM OF The BARREL!

!! CEASE !! STOP that BEASTLY DRUMMING, JEROME!
I CAN'T HELP YOU 'CAUSE I'M WORRYIN' BOUT MY FRIEND WITH NO HEAD.
I'M NOT DRUMMING, I'M PRACTICIN' EATIN'.
The boy, here, was so FEARSOMELY FORTISSIMOUS, I THOUGHT YOU said your friend had NO HEAD!!!
HOW RIDICULOUS! heh heh ??
YEAH THAT'S WHY I CAN'T THINK OF ANY TALENT; I IS SO BUSY WORRYIN'.
DID I HEAR ARIGHT, MY GOOD CHAP? THIS COMPEER, THIS COLLEAGUE OF YOURS IS HEAD-LESS?
YESSIR, MR. P.T. BRIDGEPORT.
A FOUL and FARCICAL FILLIP OF FATE! Where's he buried?
HE'S NOT.
Zounds, SIRRAH! SUCH AN INDIGNITY! And the BOARD OF HEALTH -- No Complaints ?
HE'S NOT DEAD -- HE JUST AIN'T GOT NO HEAD.
INCREASINGLY INCREDIBLE! NOT EVEN 1 ? (ONE) ?
NOT SO'S YOU'D NOTICE IT.

NOW, MY BOY, WE PICK UP THE REAR TRACK AND CARRY IT *Forward.*
YOU ONLY GOT *THREE* PIECES?
ALL MADE OF OLD *LADDERS?*
P.T.BR ORT

AH, YES, SON, *soon as we've passed over* "ONE PIECE," we put it down ahead! Thus we can go **ANYWHERE** with NO RESTRICTIONS
D.S.&F.M

HAS YOU HEARD THE **GOOD NEWS?** *P.T. BRIDGEPORT,* THE CIRCUS MAN, IS COMBIN' THE SWAMP FOR TALENT.
GREAT! I'M A ***TRAPEZE ARTIST*** BY **BIRTH!**
I EVEN **SPEAKS TRAPEZE;** LIKE THIS: *TRAP DRUM, TRAP DOOR* AN' ***TRAP, TRAP, TRAP, THE BOYS ARE MARCHIN'; HERE COMES THE GEYSER*** AT THE DOOR.
6-27

YOU CALLS **THAT** ***TRAPEZE***? WHY, YOU WOULDN'T KNOW A **AERIAL ARTISTE** IF YOU ***BIT*** ONE.
AW, I *WOULD* ***TOO***.

I COME FROM A ***LONG LINE*** OF **AERIAL ARTISTS**; I PUT UP MORE **RADIO ANTENNAS** IN 1927 THAN ***JOSEPH DZUGASHVILI,*** THE INVENTOR OF MR. R.C.A. MARCONI.

THAT POSSUM *was right as* ***RAIN***, Clarence ---
his friend *is* **HEADLESS**!

an exhilarating **EXHIBIT**! **MILLIONS IN IT!** The crowned heads of the continent will swoon --- *PRESSING* ***RUBIES*** *INTO OUR EARS!!!*

CHURCHY LAFEMME IS THE ONE WHAT MR. **P.T. BRIDGEPORT** WANTS TO PUT IN HIS **CIRCUS**.

DUNNO WHY HE'D WANT A BOY WITH **NO HEAD** - SO US BETTER GIT OL' TURTLE'S HEAD OUTEN HIS SHELL ONCE AN' FOR **ALL**.
US KIN FORCE **AIR** IN AN' **BLOW** HIS HEAD OUT ----- IS YOU ***READY***?

WHEE-- HAWKEN!
THERE HE BLOW!
I BETTER GO ON BACK IN-- I MUST OF IS LEFT MY **HAT** IN THERE SOMEPLACE.

OL' **P.T.** IS SENT ME OVER TO SIGN UP THE ***HEADLESS TURTLE*** FOR THE **CIRCUS**.

SIGN UP RIGHT AWAY AFORE MR. **BRIDGEPORT** TEARS UP THE **DOWN PAYMENT**....*NAMELY HIS* ***I.O.U.*** *FOR* ***TWENTY TWO DOLLARS.***

SIGN YO' NAME THERE.
ALL OF HER?
US FINELY GOT HIS HEAD BONE OUTEN HIS SHELL.
WHY, SO YOU IS....*I NEVER NOTICED.*
HOW YOU SPELLS "**X**"?
WITH A **7.**
NO! NO!
BUT IT'S IN HIS **CONTRACK! NO HEAD!**

WHERE IS THE HEADLESS TURTLE, Guthbert, my boy?
RIGHT AFTER I SIGNED HIM FOR OUR CIRCUS HIS HEAD POPS OUTEN HIS SHELL!

Gadzook -- and as UGLY A CRANIUM as ever has been seen -- SMALL WONDER he kept it hidden

YOU CAN'T INSULT MY PERSONAL PROPERTY.
A POX ON YOUR personal property! GET AWAY, YOU CUR! You Contract !! BREAKER!!
BUT YOU SAID I WAS GONE SEE THE WORLD ... HOW COULD I OF? ... WITH MY HEAD TUCKED AWAY?
YOU DUG YOUR SKULL OUT, ONLY AFTER THE CONTRACT WAS SIGNED ---- THAT, SIRRAH, is SKULL-DUGGERY!
-- OUT OF SEASON!

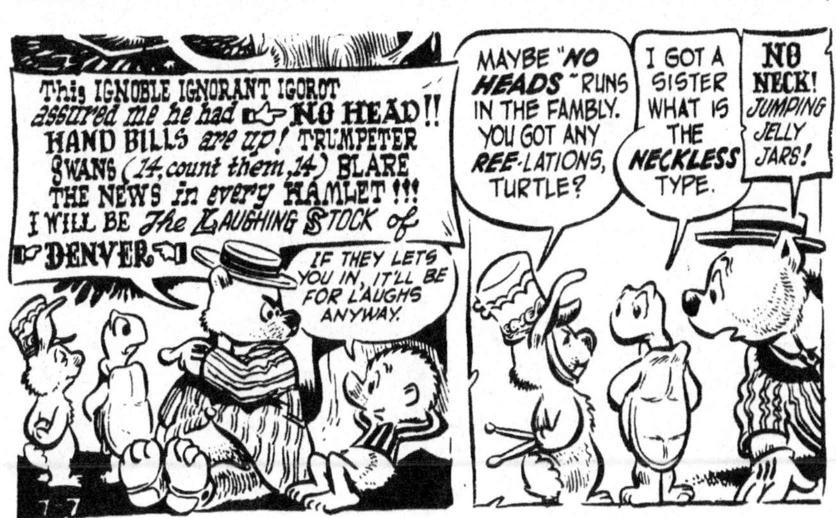
This IGNOBLE IGNORANT IGOROT assured me he had NO HEAD!! HAND BILLS are up! TRUMPETER SWANS (14, count them, 14) BLARE THE NEWS in every HAMLET!!! I WILL BE The LAUGHING STOCK of DENVER
IF THEY LETS YOU IN, IT'LL BE FOR LAUGHS ANYWAY.
7-7
MAYBE "NO HEADS" RUNS IN THE FAMBLY. YOU GOT ANY REE-LATIONS, TURTLE?
I GOT A SISTER WHAT IS THE NECKLESS TYPE.
NO NECK! JUMPING JELLY JARS!

NO... NOT NO NECK! SHE JES' LIKES NECKLESSES.. A PEARL NECKLESS... A RUBY NECKLESS... EVEN DIAMOND.. AN' AS FOR JUMPIN' JELLY JARS.... WHO CAN'T?!
SO... THAT MAKES HER A NECKLESS TYPE...
SOMEHOW I feel the SWAMP OWES ME DAMAGES!
YOU IS HAD ALL THE DAMAGES US KIN DISH OUT.. BUT, AFTER THAT DIALOGUE, I DO B'LEEVE US OWE YOU A APOLOGY.

MY BOY, I'M AFRAID THE CIRCUS of Old P.T. BRIDGEPORT is at a STULTIFYING STANDSTILL!

With the HEADLESS TURTLE having GROWN A HEAD and our FLEA CONTINGENT having ★BITTEN THE DUST★ we are without an EXHIBIT!

GONE is the SUMMER SEASON ~ THE BIG SHOW ENDS ~ THE CURTAIN FALLS ~~ Like DREAMS, WE OLD TROUPERS NEVER DIE ---- we just slowly FADE AWAY
GULP!
HERE NOW, MY BOY!! MY FINE FELLOW -- YOU'RE SPOTTING MY CRAVAT!
SURE, DON'T CRY, POGO! US SHOWBOAT TYPES TAKES ON LIKE THAT ALL THE TIME.
SOB SOB

STOP HIM, ARGENELD! STOP HIM! He's weeping a hole in my neckpiece!
BUT YOUR GOODBYE SPEECH WAS SO SAD, YOU IS BROKE HIS LI'L' HEART.
HAANH! Filiblister, my good friend, I was merely exercising my talent for the "Tender Adieu"—
YOU MEAN IT WAS ONLY YOUR FIRST FINAL FAREWELL?

My FIRST — FINAL farewell AT This or any other STAGE!
NORBERT, DO SOMETHING ABOUT THIS BLUBBERING BIBBERINE!! HE IS RUINING A TEN-CENT (10¢) FOULARD.
why, BANNISTER, my boy!
SNIMP!

FOR LACK OF OTHER ACTIVITY I THINK OUR STELLAR STUPENDOUS CIRCUS SHOULD GIVE A BENEFIT
A BENEFIT FOR WHO?

A BENEFIT SHOW THAT WOULD ENABLE YOU DENIZENS OF THE SWAMP to give succor to a DESTITUTE, FRIENDLESS and STARVING ORPHAN !!! A LONE LORN LAD ALONE IN THE WORLD. SUCH A SAD and SORRY SIGHT.

Oh, WOE! OH, WEEPFUL WAILING WOE !!
GEE, MR. BRIDGEPORT, WHO IS THIS ORPHAN WHAT US GONNA HELP?
Well, Gosh, ME (NATURALLY)

MR. P.T. BRIDGEPORT HAS PUT A SPLINT ON HIS NECKTIE AN' IS GONNA GIVE A PERFORMANCE OF THE CIRCUS FOR YOU SWAMP CRITTURS
BUT I THOUGHT HE DIDN'T HAVE ANYTHING LEFT FOR A SHOW.
STEP OVER TO THE TRAIN AN' SEE ....

HEY, C'MON OUT-- I GOT A SURPRISE FOR YOU.

FOOD?
P.T. BRIDGEPORT.

A FEW STARS AND SOME STRIPES

POGO, THIS IS **MR. TAMMANANY**, A NATURAL BORN **TIGER** BY TRADE AN' HE WORKS FOR OUR **CIRCUS** ..
GOSH, *WHERE'D HE* COME FROM?

WELL, I COME BY THE **DENVER, SEATTLE** AND **FORT MUDGE** RAILWAY FROM UP ***DEE-TROIT*** WAY ---- USED TO PLAY THE OUTFIELD.

BUT .. THE BASEBALL MEN . SUSPECTED ME OF EATING **SNACKS** BETWEEN MEALS SO I WAS RELEASED .....

GOSH ---- WHAT STRICT TRAINING RULES!

WEREN'T THEY? BUT, IT **IS** HARD TO PLAY WITHOUT AN **UMPIRE** AN' ***GEORGE Z. SNACKS*** WAS A HOME PLATE MAN THAT ***EVERYONE*** LIKED ---- ***I*** DID, ***MYSELF*** ... A MAN OF **EXCELLENT TASTE**.

POGO IS GONE THROW A LI'L' PARTY FOR YOU, MR. TAMMANANY
WELL, NOW THAT'S JUST DELICIOUS OF HIM.
I THREW A PARTY IN THE POTOMAC ONCE 'BOUT TWENTY YEARS BACK! BIGGEST SOCIAL SPLASH OF THE SEASON.
HERE, MR. TAMMANANY

THANKS, PASS THE MUSTARD, ADELBERT ----
HEY! HEY! THAT'S NOT POLITE --- HE'S YOUR HOST.
HEY! I DON'T LIKE MUSTARD!
GOLLY! WHAT A MISTAKE YOU COULD OF MADE!
I'LL SAY, KID... IT WOULD HAVE BEEN BAD! RAW MEAT GIVES ME HICCUPS SOMETHING FIERCE .... I'D HAVE BEEN AWAKE ALL NIGHT.
THAT'D BE TOUGH
WHILE US IS POKIN' AT THE FISH, YOU COULD GIT MORE WOOD, MR. TAMMANANY
WOOD?! WHO WANTS TO EAT WOOD?
IT'S FOR THE FIRE... DON'T GET SCARED IN THE WOODS NOW.
PHOOMPH! TIGERS ARE SIMPLY FEARLESS.

SIMPLY FEARLESS, YESSIR, ABSOLUTELY WITHOUT FEAR OF MAN OR BEAS- YOW HELP!
ROWF ROWF
GET THIS MONSTER OFF -- HE'S KILLIN' ME.
I TOLE THE PUP-DOG AN' I TOLE HIM ---- DON'T CHASE CATS, I SAID.
IF THAT CIRCUS TIGER, NAME OF MR. TAMMANANY, AIN'T A-COMIN', US MOUGHT'S WELL PROCEED.
MOUGHT'S WELL.
ROWF ROWF ROWF ROWF ROWF ROWF ROWF ROWF ROWF ROWF ROWF
HELP!

FACINOROUS RUNAGATES!
YEAH!
COME BACK COME BACK COME BACK COME BACK COME BACKCOMEBACKCOMEBACK!
I TOLE THAT PUPDOG AN I TOLE HIM --" DON'T CHASE CATS!" I TOLE HIM ----- THAT'S WHAT I TOLE HIM ...
GOO-OOD FOR YOU!

HERE COMES MR. TAMMANANY BACK FROM HIS LI'L' RUN.
DID THAT SMALL SIZED DOG GIT TIRED OF CHASIN' YOU?
WELL, SIRS, THAT PUP.DOG HAS FORMED QUITE AN ATTACHMENT FOR ME!

AND YOU FOR HIM?
UM--MM--- IT DO KINDA WORK BOTH WAYS.
?

FACT IS.... HE WON'T LET GO!

THE WAY TO GET THE PUP DOG TO LET GO IS TO CAUSE A SNEEZE. SO I'LL SHAKE THIS PEPPER ON HIM AN---
GREAT... GREAT!

AH-CHOO!

Gesundheit!

CONGRATULATIONS.

SO, YOU'VE MET MY ASSISTANT, the TIGER?
YEP, HE'S IN GETTIN' READY FOR THE CIRCUS REHEARSAL.
I SHOULD TELL YOU MORE ABOUT THAT DETROIT UMPIRE, NAMED SNACKS, A MAN OF RARE PERCEPTION.
That's him — LOVELY VOICE, eh? I'd use him for a SOPRANO LEAD if he didn't TAKE The PART OF A LION!
LION?

IN FACT, SNACKS HAD SUCH RARE PERCEPTIONS THEY AMOUNTED TO HALLUCINATIONS. I RECALL ONE TIME WE HAD FIVE MEN ON BASE AND HE SAID WE COULDN'T HAVE MORE THAN TWO ON FOURTH — WELL, SIR, YOU CAN BET....
GEE, WHY NOT USE HIM PLAIN? LIKE A TIGER.
EXCELLENT SUGGESTION — AND IF YOU'D STOP THAT INFERNAL DRUMMING, SEBASTION, YOU, TOO, MIGHT HAVE AN IDEA ON OCCASION!!
I GOT ONE, BUT I AIN'T GONE SAY.

BEHOLD! I Present the BLOOD CURLING LEON the LION
AW, THAT'S JUST OL' TAMMANANY, THE TIGER; --- SEE HIS STRIPES?
HEY HEY
VERY WELL, KEEP YOUR SEATS, FOLKS!

BEHOLD!
A ZEBRA --- a zebra -- A REAL FOUR {COUNT THEM} FOUR LEGGED --

ZEBRA --? BEHOLD? YOO HOO, BEHOLD, PLEASE?
LOOKY AT HIM WINGLE HIS EARS.
DO IT AGIN, RACKETY COON CHILE.

The GREAT SHOW IS A FAILURE -- I'M RUINED -- RUINED! A Small boy wiggling his ears OUTDRAWS US!

I'M DESPERATE ---- I'D BEST STEP INTO THE COOL HERE AND CALM MY THOUGHTS.
HEY... WAIT!

YOU SNEEPIN' TOM! POKIN' IN WHEN I IS DE-ROBED!
THER' WAS A TIME WHEN THE LAW ALLOWED US PO'R WIDDER WIMMEN THE RIGHT OF PRIVATE ASSEMBLY.
THAT WAS DESPRIT... MIZ BEAVER WAS IN THERE TAKIN' A BATH.

TAMMANANY, I'M AFRAID YOU'LL HAVE TO ACCEPT YOUR WALKING PAPERS.
WHERE YOU WANT ME TO WALK?
The CIRCUS is done --- I'M GOING to CONVERT THE TRAIN into a Lunch Wagon.
YOU'RE ALL SET FOR A WAGON, WHAT ARE YOU DOIN' FOR LUNCH?
NOT A THING -- I accept your invitation with thanks.
EASE OFF. YOU JUST GAVE ME THE SACK, REMEMBER?
Well, it's your OWN FAULT --- if you'd been able to take the part of a LION, we'd be booming today---
IT'S BEEN MY EXPERIENCE THAT A LION CAN TAKE HIS OWN PART --

WELL, I'M HITTING THE ROAD, POGO; THE CIRCUS HAS FOLDED, YES...

...HAS FOLDED ITSELF LIKE AN OLD A-RAB AND SILENTLY FADES AWAY-----MR. BRIDGEPORT IS BACK THERE LEARNING THE TIGHT ROPE, WORKING FOR A COMEBACK, BUT...

SPLAP!
AS FOR ME, I'M NOT THE SORT TO GAMBLE. I'M THE STEADY KIND...
WHERE AS THE SHOWBOAT TYPE LIKE MR. P.T. IS ALWAYS HOPING FOR THE BIG DAILY DOUBLE PLAY. HE'S CONTENT TO TINKER FOR EVER WITH CHANCE.
Help! I SAY, HELP! YOO HOO?
BUT YOU PREFERS STEADY UNEMPLOYMENT.

WHAT YOU FIGGERIN' ON DOIN' IF YOU GOES OUT OF THE CIRCUS TIGERIN' BUSINESS, MR. TAMMANANY?
WELL, THERE'S A BIG SOCIAL PARTY UP IN NEW YORK COULD USE A LITTLE MUSCLE... OR, OF 'COURSE A BOY WITH AS MANY STRIPES AS ME WOULD DO WELL IN THE NAVY....

WELL, FRIENDS, I'M ON MY WAY...
I TRUST, TAMMANANY, That you will broadcast the FAME of my NEW Lunchwagon...
HOW CAN I? YOU HASN'T HAD ANY FOOD IN IT YET!
Phaw! Your CRASS COMMERCIALISM is COMMON CURMUDGERY! Yesterday we had a EGG

SO... HOW DID YOU COOK IT?
COOK IT?! HAVE YOU NO Mother Instinct? IT HATCHED!
AND YOU LEFT IT ALONE TODAY? UNPROTECTED... NOT EVEN A BABY SITTER?
SIR, THERE is a WORD for You....
CHEEP!
IT GOT YOUR EYES, P.T.

P.T., I DON'T SUPPOSE YOU WANT TO GO WITH ME?
YOU CAN SEE my hands are TIED!
SINCE THE EGG hatched I am BOUND HERE by TIES TOO STRONG for the TUG of ADVENTURE TO BREAK.
CHEEP?

COOTCHIE COO?
HEAR THAT? ISN'T THAT DISGUSTIN'? HE'S PASSIN' UP A CHANCE TO WIN FAME AND FORTUNE.

'CAUSE HE'S AN ADULT HE'S GONNA BE A FAMILY MAN AND WILL SPEND THE REST OF HIS LIFE BEIN' TIED DOWN AN' NERVOUS AN' WORRIED ----AN' THE TROUBLE IS: HE'LL BE SO HAPPY ABOUT IT.
WHARF.

I'M NOT TAKIN' ANY CHANCES ON GROWIN' UP AN' HAVIN' FIFTY OR SIXTY CHILDREN ....

THE BEST THING TO DO IS RUN OFF NOW WHILE I'M SPRY AN' YOUNG AN' SCHOOL IS OUT .... MM-MM
HUNKABERRY

AN' SEEK MY FORTUNE AN NOT GET ALL TANGLED AND TURMOILED ...

AN' TOP HEAVIED WITH THINGS THAT ONLY SLOW A MAN UP.
WURF.

TIGER RAGOUT

MR. TAMMANANY IS HITTIN' THE ROAD TOO, SO DON'T YOU GO CHASIN' HIM IF WE SEE HIM....

JUST CAUSE *YOU* DON'T LIKE *CATS*... *OOP! THERE HE IS!*
RALPH
RALPH
RALPH
RALPH

COME BACK! COME BACK!
OW!
CRUNCH!

DID HE HURT YOU? *WHERE'D HE BITE YOU?*
HE BIT ME ON THE TUCKERBAG AN' MY CURIOS AN' VALUABLES IS LEAKIN'!

CATS AN' DOGS IS *TRADITIONARY* ENEMIES SO PUP-DOG GOTTA CHAW UP MY TAILBONE.
HE'S KINDA RELENTLESS IN THIS RESPECK.
RRRRRRRRRRRRRR

YOU KNOW THE PO'R SCAPER GOT A PEAKIED LOOK FROM TROTTIN' 'LONG CARRYIN' MY ACCOUTERMINTS.

MEBBE THERE'S A GEWGAW IN THE TUCKERBAG WHAT'LL HELP OUT...

THERE'S NO SENSE IN RUNNIN' AWAY FROM HOME IN DISCOMFORT....MM Muss i denn, Muss i denn zum— Städt·le hin-aus Städt·le hin-aus, und du mein Schatz, bleibst hier!

A NOISE!
A NOISE?
CRACK! CRACK!

BEST THING TO HAVE 'TWEEN YOU AN' WILD ANIMALS IS FIRE...
AN HEIGHT
CRIK

AN' HEIGHT!
CRACK!
HARRUMPH!

LOOK AHEAD, LOOK ASTERN, LOOK THE WEATHER IN THE LEE. BLOW HIGH, BLOW LOW... WELL! WHAT'S COOKIN', MATES?

SO YOU'RE JUST A MOUSE.
WODDYA MEAN JUST? GEE, I'M GLAD TO SEE THE PUP-DOG AGAIN ...HIM AN' ME SERVED A HITCH IN TH' POKEY TOGETHER LAST YEAR...
...ON ACCOUNT THEY HUNG A FRAME ON US.
YOU WERE INNOCENT?

ON THIS PARTICULAR RAP, WE WAS AS CLEAN AS NEW BORNED BABES, WHICH THE HOUND HERE, AT THE TIME, WAS, INDEED. IT WAS DISGRACEFUL.
DISGRACEFUL?
A PROFESSIONAL INSULT, AND A VIOLATION OF MY RIGHTS, TO BE JUGGED FOR A STUPID CRIME I HADN'T DONE WHEN THE CRIMES I HAVE DONE ARE SO MUCH MORE FASCINATIN'...... BUT... MODESTY PRE-VAILED AND...
AW, YOU OL' PUP-DOG, YOU.

PERHAPS YOU'D CARE TO JOIN US FOR A VOYAGE OF SONG, FORTUNE SEEKING AN' GENERAL CULTIVATION.
I AIN'T MUCH FOR CULTIVATIN' GENERALS, BUT I'VE NAVY TRAININ' ...OF THE LOOSE SHIP VARIETY.

WE'RE ALL SET.... READY TO VENTURE FORTH!
HAVE WE GOT EVERYTHING? MATCHES ... KNIVES, FORKS...
YEP... CAN OPENER... FRYIN' PAN ... HAND AX ..
CUPS PAPER PLATES YEP-EVER'THING.

FOOD?
FOOD?
OH... FOOD.
MIGHT BE A GOOD IDEA TO HAVE A LITTLE ALONG. WHEN YOU STARVE WITH A TIGER, THE TIGER STARVES LAST.
I DON'T KNOW AS I CARE FOR CERTAIN MICE.
MMM... JUST MICE?

WELL, LET'S DECIDE ON THE FOOD WE'LL NEED ... I LOVES PANCAKES AN' PUP-DOG ENJOYS BONES.
MOUSE IMPLIED I WAS A CANNIBAL.
I'M PARTIAL TO CHEESE.

CANNIBALS EAT THEIR OWN KIND... DOES YOU WANT US TO GET A COUPLA TENDER TIGERS FOR YOU?
I HEAR TELL ALL TIGERS ARE MAN-EATERS.

DO HE MEAN THE HUMAN TYPE OF MAN?
THEY'RE SCARCE NOW, BUT MARK HIM DOWN FOR A FEW SMALL ONES
I HARDLY BELIEVE IN 'EM --- IS THEY REALLY REAL? I BETS THEY'D GIT UGLY IF YOU ET AT 'EM ...
WELL, THEY IS A LITTLE UNREAL AN' LAND KNOWS THEY'RE UGLY ENOUGH.
LET 'EM KEEP ON EATIN' THEIR OWN SELFS --- I'M GOIN TO SCARE UP SOME PORK AN' BEANS.

AH! MIZ BEAVER, I BELIEVE.
YOU GIT ON BACK TO THE ROAD GANG, JAILBIRD 'FORE I SPOIL'S YO' PERTY SUIT.
OH, I'M ONLY A TIGER .. LOOKING FOR FOOD FOR SOME FRIENDS ...
WELL, STEP OVER TO MY LADIES' AID MEETIN' ... WE'LL SEE WHAT WE CAN DO.

I'M SO HUNGRY I COULD EAT A WHOLE COW .... HORNS AND BELL ...

OOMP ...
BY BILLY BOWLEGS! I'M INSULTED!
SLOWLEE! SUCH A TASTES COULD BE ZE COMPLEEMENT.
I HOPE THAT WAS MERE A FIGMENT OF SPEECH

THE TIGER GOIN' OFF TO LOOK FOR FOOD REMINDS ME OF A TIME WE WAS FORAGIN' FOR GRUB DURIN' THE BOXER REBELLION ....

ME AN' ANOTHER MEMBER OF THE CAVALRY, A FELLOW WHO WAS A HORSE AT THE TIME, CAME UPON A FINE FAT ELEPHANT WHICH WAS JUST WAITIN' TO BE EATEN... WELL, SIR, WE QUIETLY CARVED IT INTO STEAKS IN MY TENT ONE NIGHT BETWEEN VESPERS AN' TAPS,

WHEN MY COMPANION RECALLED HE WAS A VEGETARIAN... RATHER'N HAVE HIM BREAK HIS VOWS, I HAD TO EAT THE WHOLE WORKS..... I'M FINISHIN', SEE, WHEN IN COMES THE SARGE...."YOU CHAPS SEEN OUR NEW COMMANDER?" HE ASKS ----

"FELLOW IN A GREY SUIT.. GOT A FIERCE LONG TRUNK ON HIM!"... WELL, YOU CAN IMAGINE HOW I FELT --- TAR TAKE THEM KINGFISHERS! THEY'RE THICKER'N SWAMP-WATER COFFEE.

WHY, HEY, THERE, OL PIGEON! THOUGHT YOU WAS IN WASHINGTON. DID YOU SEE A KINGFISHER WHAT STOLE A FISH FROM MY FRIEND, THE MOUSE?

HELLO, SON! NO, NOT NOW. MAYBE I DID. DID HE INDEED?

I'M TEACHIN' YOUNG FOLKS TO FLY AN' IT SEEM LIKE I DO GOT A KINGFISHER TAD IN THE CLASS. HEY, AL! AL!

ALCYON, YOU BRING BACK THE MAN'S PROPERTY AND PUT IT DOWN HERE IMMEDIATE!
OH, ALL RIGHT.
IS THAT THE SAME FISH?
'FRAID SO... IT DIDN'T HOLD UP SO GOOD.

WHAT IS THAT BOOK YOU GOT THERE, MR. PIGEON?
THIS HERE IS "CAPTAIN WIMBY'S NATIVE BIRD ATLAS", WHAT I'M USIN' TO LEARN THIS YOUNG SPRAT HOW TO ACT.
CAPTAIN WIMBY
IT SAYS: "The song of the Kingfisher is a loud harsh rattle." OKAY, GIVE IT A TRY, ALCYON. HERE'S YOUR KEY.
BABY WEAR
ME? RATTLE?
CAPTAIN WIMBY'S NATIVE

RATTLE INDEED! WHAT KIND OF A BIRD SONG IS THAT? WHAT IS HE, A OLD AUTOMOBILE? STEP OVER HERE, SON, I'LL TEACH YOU A SNAPPY NUMBER I PICKED UP IN SINGAPORE.
GOOD, 'CAUSE AT RATTLIN' I'M TONE DEATH.
HERE NOW!
"OH, MAMIE MINDED MAMMA, 'TIL ONE DAY IN SINGAPORE, A SAILORMAN FROM TURKESTAN CAME KNOCKIN' AT THE DOOR.
I NEED A HAT FOR THIS.

IT AIN'T MY PERSONAL OPINION THAT THE KID, ALCYON, IS GONNA SHAPE UP SO GOOD AS A KINGFISHER. HE DON'T LIKE BAITIN' THE HOOK AND HE CAN'T MEMORIZE HIS BIRDSONG.
YOU TAUGHT HIM A MUSIC HALL ROWDY-DO WITH FOREIGN PHRASES, THAT'S WHY.
CAPTAIN WIMBY'S
I'LL LOOK UP 'BOUT KING-FISHERS AGAIN. "It eats ants and POISON IVY BERRIES. Its call is Wicker! Wicker!" TRY THAT, ALCYON.
CAPTAIN WIMBY'S NATIVE BIRD ATLAS

I'LL TRY THE HOLLER, BUT I'M NOT EATIN' NO ANTS AN' POISON IVY..... WICKER! NOTHIN' TO IT. WICKER! WICKER!
HAVE YOU NO RESPECT FOR CAPTAIN WIMBY?
HOLD IT! HOLD IT!
CAPTAIN WIMBY'S
LOOK, YOU WAS READIN' 'BOUT YALLER SHAFTED FLICKERS.... MUST OF SKUP A PAGE.
MUST OF DID.
'CEPT FER THE DIET AN' THEM YALLER SHAFTS I WOULDN'T MIND FLICKERIN'.
IF YOU CAN'T CONCENTRATE ON BEIN' A KINGFISHER, THE ATLAS DESCRIBES A DELIGHTFUL BIRD TO BE; IT IS UNUSUALLY COMMON IN MANGROVE THICKETS...
HOLD IT, AGAIN!
I DONT THINK THIS UNSPOILED YOUTH OUGHT TO BE COMMON IN OR OUT OF A MANGROVE THICKET.
WISE COUNSEL! WELL, THEN HOW ABOUT BE IN' A BLACKWHISKERED VIREO?
SUITS ME. WHAT'S HE DO?

EATS SEEDS.... AN' ITS SONG IS IN BROKEN FOUR NOTE PHRASES SOUNDING LIKE "WHIP-TOM-KELLY," OR "JOHN-TO-WHIT" OR "CHEAP JOHN-STIR-UP!"
HOP-MY-TOADS! I'D BE THE LAUGHIN' STOCK OF WARE COUNTY!
YOU GOT ANY OBJECTION TO TEACHIN' ME TO BE A MOUSE?
WITH WINGS? AND FEATHERS? I'D BE DRUMMED OUTEN THE LODGE.

I MUST GET BACK TO MY FRIENDS. WE HAVE TO HIT THE ROAD
OH, ONCE I DREAMED OF GOING WEST WHERE THE GLISTEN OF THE SIX-GUN LIGHTS THE TRAIL.
BUT I CAN'T MAKE A NOISE LIKE A COW. ALL I CAN HOLLER IS: "MEOW!" SO I WENT OFF TO FORT MUDGE TO CHASE MICE.

HOWEVER, A CAT ABOUT TWO INCHES HIGH, WEARING A DERBY, CONVINCED ME THERE WAS NO FUTURE IN IT---HE SOLD ME A HALF-INTEREST IN A MILK ROUTE --- LET ME PULL THE WAGON, BUT ---.
A CAT! IN A DERBY!?
SMOKIN' A CIGAR? GREY FUR? LONG SKINNY TAIL? BIG PINK EARS? HOW'D YOU KNOW HE WAS A CAT?
HE MEOWED TOO...VERY FOND OF CHEESE. WHY? YOU KNOW HIM?

SOME **HEAVYFOOTED SOMETHIN'** IS FOOTIN' IT OUR WAY.
CLUMP! CLUMP! CLOP!

IT'S A ***WESTERN CHAPARRAL COCK!*** A **ROADRUNNER!**
CLOMP! CLOP CLUMP!
63

ANYBODY HEADIN' ME? OLD **C.C.** TOLD ME THE ***TRANSCONTINENTAL MARATHON*** WOULD GO THIS WAY... ***I'M*** OUT IN FRONT, FAR AS I KNOW.
GEE, MR. PYLE'S ***BUNION DERBY*** ENDED ABOUT **TWENTY YEAR BACK.**
DON'T THAT BEAT ALL? THEY BEEN KEEPIN' IT A SECRET! 'FRAID TO ADMIT THEY QUIT... ***BY NED, IF I'D KNEWN THAT I WOULDN'T OF HURRIED!***
63
63

WISH THAT OL' ***TIGER'D*** COME BACK... I'M TIRED OF TRYIN' TO EDUCATE KING-FISHERS, AND THIS ROADRUNNER FROM OUT WEST IS LOOSE IN THE FLUE.
HE JUST REALIZED THE **C.C. PYLE** BUNION DERBY WAS OVER? ***WHAT HAPPENED?***
SAID HE WAS MAKIN' GOOD TIME BUT HEADED WRONG. HE WOUND UP IN ***MANITOBA*** ...TURNED AROUND AND FOUND HIMSELF IN **ECUADOR.**

GOT RUNNIN' ABSENTMINDED-LIKE AFTER THAT AN' NOTICED HE WAS IN A PUB IN LIVERPOOL ... THINKS HE MIGHT OF BEEN THE ONLY MAN TO RUN ACROSS THE ENGLISH CHANNEL BECAUSE HE FOUND A COUPLA FRENCH SOUS IN HIS .... HEY!
ALLRIGHT, CUT THE COMEDY! YOU GOT A LICENSE, JACK?

I BEEN TRYIN' TO TEACH LI'L' ALCYON HERE TO BE A KINGFISHER BUT HE DON'T LIKE IT.
HE LOOKS BRIGHT ENOUGH AND I COULD USE SOME HELP.
HOW'D YOU LIKE TO BE AN APPRENTICE ROADRUNNER, KIDDO? YOU'D GET TO TRAVEL.
SOUNDS PEACHY.

CAPTAIN WIMBY'S BIRD ATLAS SAYS: The spring song of the Roadrunner is "Kook-ook-ook-ook-ook-ook-ook-" RUNNIN' DOWN THE SCALE.
THAT RUNS DOWN THE WHOLE MUSIC INDUSTRY... WIMBY ISN'T EXACTLY AN OSCAR HAMMERSTEIN, IS HE?
SOME LYRICS!
LET ORNITHOLOGISTS WRITE THE RULES SO LONG AS WE CAN WRITE THE SONGS... IF YOU KEEP MOVIN', KID, YOU CAN SING AS YOU PLEASE.

WELL, WE'RE OFF, ALCYON, AN' I KNOW YOU'LL MAKE A GOOD ROADRUNNER.
GOOD, 'CAUSE THEY BUILDS NESTS LOW DOWN, AN' I AIN'T GITTIN' UP IN NO TREES.
GOODBYE GOODBYE
AS I WAS SAYIN', MR. TAMMANANY, THIS CAT IN FORT MUDGE PERSUADED ME TO NOT CHASE MICE. HE WORE A DERBY, SMOKED A CIGAR AN' SAID, "MEOW," LIKE ME.
SOMEBODY A-COMIN'.

GOIN' SOMEPLACE?
HEY, YOU! WAIT!
NOTHIN' TO SAY, RODENT? CAT GOT YOUR TONGUE?
ME-OW DO YOU DO?

MY SAKES! SO YOU ARE A MOUSE! AND YOU MADE BELIEVE YOU WERE A CAT.
PHMF! NOT SO FELICITOUS TO THE FAMILY FELIDAE.
WELL, I WAS AFRAID YOU'D EAT ME OUT OF HOUSE, HOME AN' ME.
EAT MICE? HOW VERY UNAPPETIZING!

WHAT'S SO UNAPPETIZING ABOUT MICE, COME TO THINK OF IT?
WHY'D YOU DECIDE TO BE A CAT, ANYWAY?
'CAUSE I CAN ONLY HOLLER "MEOW."... CAN'T MAKE THE COW-CRY.
NOTHIN' TO IT... MOO...OOO... HOW'S THAT?
LOVELY!
SOUNDS LIKE THE START OF A GREAT TEAM.

SO YOU'RE GOIN' OUT WEST AND HELP HORRORS GREELEY TO MOO?
YEP, AN' HERE'S A LITTLE KEEPSAKE FROM YOUR OLD TIGER PAL.
MIND! YOU CHILDREN GO STRAIGHT HOME.

IF YOU'RE GOIN' TO BE A COWBOY, YOU CAN'T CRY, MR. TAMMANANY.
WHO'S CRYIN'? I HAD A LUMP IN MY THROAT AND IT GOT IN MY EYE.
GOODBYE, Y'ALL! YOU COME SEE US REAL SOON NOW... --HEAR? SAY...THIS KEEPSAKE IS GOT TWO HEADS ON IT.

The SAFER SAFARI

IS YOU REALLY GONE TAKE UNCIVIL LIBERTIES WITH MR. TAMMANANY, THE TIGER, BY SHOOTIN' HIM ON SIGHT?
MAN! YOU CAN'T SHOOT HIM AHEAD OF THAT----- AN' HE MUST OF ET THE RACKETY-COON CHILE ... BOTH IS GONE!
AN' THE PUP-DOG, TOO.
IT'S UTMOST INCREDIBOBBLE THAT HE'D EAT THE PUP-DOG
MM... DOGMEAT AIN'T GENERALLY TOO SAVOIR A FARE.
SIR?
OOP! DIN'T MEAN NOTHIN' PERSONIAL.. I BE GLAD TO EAT YOU IF YOU GONE STEW 'BOUT IT....
WE IS GONE TRACK DOWN THE TIGER WHAT UNDOUBTABOBBLY ATE THE YOUNG UNS.
AN' HE IS GONE BE COMPLETELY SHOT AT!
DON'T FERGIT YOU IS DEE-PRIVIN' HIM OF HIS RIGHTS IF YOU LYNCHES HIM THIS WAY.

WHY, SON, HOW YOU DO GO ON --- WE ISN'T DEE-PRIVIN' HIM OF NO RIGHTS, NO HOW!
HE GOT A PERFECK RIGHT TO BE LYNCHED.....
HE'S JES' AS GOOD AS ANYBODY ELSE.

PORKY, GIT OUT THE MEDICAL CHEST. ALBERT IS GOT A LOADED GUN!
I'D RATHER GIT OUT OF TOWN.

I TOLE ALBERT AN' I TOLE HIM, "DON'T GO SHOOT THE TIGER JES' 'CAUSE YOU 'SPECT HE ET THE RACKETY-COON CHILE." THAT'S WHAT I TOLE HIM.
DON'T HE RECALL BEIN' ACCUSED OF EATIN' FOLKS HIS OWN NATURAL-BORN SELF?
BRRRRRRR YEP... BUT HE SAY IT ALLUS WAS PERFECT CLEAR TO HIM THAT HE WAS INNOCENT.
SO HE WOULDN'T OF SHOT HIS SELF?

NOPE! BUT NOW THE POSSE IS LOADED FOR TIGER...SO US BETTER TAG 'LONG AND PICK UP THE PIECES.
DIN'T YOU TURN YOUR BIG OL' BROWN COLORED EYE BALLS ON HIM AND APPEAL TO HIS BETTER INSTINCTS?
OH, YEP! BUT HE ACCUSE ME OF INNERFEARIN' WITH HIS NATURAL BORN INSTINCT TO DISREGARD 'EM.
WELL, YOU GOTTA RESPECT A MAN'S SPECIAL PRIVILEGES IN THIS HERE WORLD... HERE! GIT OFF! NO HINGE-HIKERS!
CHEAPSCAPES!

I'LL LOOK FOR MORE FIRE WOOD WHILST THE JUNIOR LEAGUE PREPARES THE GRUB.

HAW! FUNNY HOW THAT OL' COW COULDN'T MOO AN' KEPT CRYIN': "MEOW"!... SO WE SAID WE WAS BOTH CATS AN' SPENT THE EVENIN' SINGIN': MEOW-MEOW-MEOW!

WHAT KIND NOISES DO TIGERS MAKE?
NOISES LIKE CATS' NOISES.
CATS?
MEE-OW MEOW

MEOW MEOW

POGO!
WHY, LI'L' MOUSE! IT SURE IS GOOD TO SEE YOU AGAIN.... IS YOU SEEN A PARCEL OF TIGER HUNTERS?
SEEMS TO ME I SPIED A FORTIFIED GROUP BEARIN' A DEE FENSE STOCKPILE OF MORTAR, DAGGER AND KNOUT BACK A PIECE --IS THEY A TIGER SAFARI?

YEP... ME AN' PORKY IS FOLLYIN' ALONG TO BANDAGE UP THE TIGER AFTER THEY SWEEPS DOWN ON HIM LIKE THE HUNGRY SIOUX.
THEY IS FIERCE?

FIERCE INDEED
AN' FEARLESS INDEED FORSOOTH BESIDES.
YOU BETTER HURRY, THEY WAS FALLIN' OUTEN THE TREE THEY WAS HIDIN' IN WHEN I PASSED. THEY'LL NEED SPLINTS ON THEIR FLINT-LOCKS.

NOW THE FIRST THING US TIGER HUNTERS GOTTA DO IS LEARN TO RECOGNIZE THIS TIGER.
NOBLE SPOKE.
I'D RECOGNIZE HIM EASY... I WAS HOPIN' HE WOULDN'T RECOGNIZE ME.
US CAN'T KEEP GITTIN' PANICKY WHEN US HEARS HIS ROAR.
ME OW!
HIS ROAR AGAIN.
SPINE CURDLIN'!

THE BLOOD STARIN' ROAR OF A SAVAGE MAN-EATER.
LISTEN AT HIM GNASH AN' GNARL HIS TEETH!
MEOW.
OH... H'LO, MIZ CATBIRD
NICE DAY.
H'LO, ALBERT,
NOW TRY IT AGIN, PEMBERWYCK, SON; YOU IS LEARNIN' FIRST RATE.
MEE OW ME OW ME-OW.
FELLOW TIGER HUNTERS, US GOTTA MOVE FORWARD REELENTLESS AN' IRREGARDLESS!
RIGHT RIGHT RIGHT RIGHT RIGHT RIGHT RIGHT RIGHT
NO MORE SOFT-HEARTIN' IT. I IS LOADIN' MY GUN AN' THE NEXT TIGER NOISE US HEARS: BLAM!
BLAM, SIR?
BLAM IT IS.... I IS-UM-- UH--SORTA HANDSTRUNG, HERE.
STUCK, EH?
IF I WAS AT THEM CONTROLS I COULD PULL THE TRIGGER AN-....
GIT AWAY! 'FORE I IS DES-PRIT ENUFF TO USE YO' BRAINS I'D USE MY OWN.

I KNOW THIS: IF THAT RACKETY-COON CHILE ISN'T BEEN ET BY THE TIGER, HE SURE GONE CATCH IT WHEN HE GIT ON HOME.
AN' THE PUPDOG, TOO, IS BEEN RUNNED-AWAY FROM HOME TOO LONG! BE GONE BEAT BUMPS ON HIS BONE HEAD!
GOOD OL' MOSS.

HOWDY, STRANGERS.
HUM... H'LO, STRANGERS. IS YOU SEED A TIGER?
YEP! A BULL-SIZE BATCH OF 'EM IS OVER 'HIND THE HILL A-HUNTIN' OF ALLIGORATOR.
MAN! THAT LI'L' PUPPY TYPE DOG MUST IS OVER A HUNNERD YEAR OLD!

HOWDY, STRANGERS.
HOWDY, STRANGERS.... IS YOU SEED ANY TIGER HUNTERS?

NO SPEAK ENGLISH.
WHY NOT?

'CAUSE US IS NEW-BORNED FOREIGN TYPE OF REFUGEES AN' GOT NO UNCLE SAM.
YOU CONVINCES ME! WHAT LANGUAGE IS YOU SPEAKIN'? SEEM LIKE I UNDERSTAN'S HER PERTY GOOD.
TOVARISCH! WHAT YOU KNOW?! WE IS RUNNED ACROSS A SLEIGHFUL OF OUR COUNTRY-MEN! THEY TALKS LATIN, TOO!
LET'S ALL ROOM TO-GETHER NEXT TERM.
CAVE CANEM

WHO ALL IS LOOKIN' FOR THE RACKETY-COON CHILE AN' THE PUP-DOG, UNCLE POGO? I MEAN STRANGER.
WELL, STRANGER, EVER'BODY INCLUDIN' YO' PAP,...I MEAN MR. RACKETY-COON... AN' US IS SPREAD PERTY THIN, STRANGER.
A FEW IS HUNTIN' IN THE HOLLER.. MORE IS STOMPIN' 'ROUND BOWLEG'S ISLAND... BOATS IS PLYIN' THE DARK WATERS
NOT 'NUFF MEN TO SAIL 'EM-- SO EACH GOT A SKELETON CREW.

A SKELETON CREW?
SKELETON
WHOO! I IS FOUND NOW! CALL OFF THEM BONEYARD BIRDS!
I DECLARE! I IS NEVER BEEN MORE SURPRISED!
NEITHER IS ME!

36 HOURS AND 253 HUSH PUPPIES LATER.

I SAID I BET...
'SCUSE ME AGIN.... STOP PLAYIN' STAGE COACH!
BANG BANG! BANG
BUT WE DOOD LIKE YOU SAY! NOW US IS THE U.S. CAVALARY SAVIN' THE FORT.
BUT, TO PLEASE YOU, US'LL STOP PLAYIN' THAT AN' MERE TAKE A LI'L' TARGET PRACTICE...
BANG! BANG! BANG! BANG!
WHAT IS YOU SAYIN', POGO?
NAUGHT.

US WILL JES' GOTTA REPORT THAT THE RACKETY-COON CHILE AN' THE PUP-DOG IS GONE!
PROBABOBBLY EATEN.
WHAT WILL US EVER TELL THE TAD'S KINFOLK WHEN THEY GITS ON HOME?
MR. RACKETY C
SPSSssST.... YOU WANNA PLAY COWBOY?
SNRRFF! GULP...SNF. DON'T MIND IF I DO.

BANG! BANG! BAA-KAHAOW! KAH-H-HAOW! BANG!
ISN'T YOU SPRATS GOT NO SENSE OF REE-SPECT?
WHAT IS A-BITIN' OF HIM?
SHH.... I FORGOT. US IS CRYIN'... SOMEBODY GOT DEAD.
LOAN ME THE BORRY OF YO' HANKY ONCE AN' A WHILE
SNULF

OH, WEEPIN' WAILFUL WOE!
WHAT'S Y'ALL A-BLUBBERIN' UP MY FRONT STEP FOR?
OH, MR. RACKETY-COON, US THREE TIGER HUNTERS IS GOT...
THREE? LOOKS LIKE FOUR OF YOU.

LET'S BE FAIR... I'LL SKRINCH OVER HERE TO GIT YO' VIEWPOINT... ONE-TWO-THREE IS ALL I SEE.
ALBERT, YOU COULDN'T COUNT WATER IN A BUCKET.
I KIN TOO! AN' I KIN COUNT US TIGER HUNTERS WITH OUT LOOKIN'... ONE-TWO-THREE IT IS!
YOU HAVE A EYE-TEST LATELY, SIR?
ONE-TWO BUCKLE MY SHOE THREE-FOUR... I KEEP GITTIN' 19

I GOT A GOOD MIND TO NEVER SPEAK TO ANYBODY AGAIN.
ALBERT, WHEN YOU COUNTED THE TIGER HUNTERS YOU DIN'T COUNT YO'SELF, SO YOU GOT THREE BY LEAVIN' ONE OUT.
?
BUT ACTUAL YOU SHOULD OF LEFT OUT MY TAD HERE 'CAUSE HE WASN'T NO TIGER HUNTER....

WAIT NOW! YOU COUNTED FOUR.... NOW TWO IS LEFT OUT---SO THEY'S ONLY TWO OF US!?
WORSE! HE PROVED THEY WAS ONLY THREE OF US AT FIRST...SO TAKIN' TWO OUT MEANS THEY IS ONLY ONE OF US!
WE BETTER HOLD HANDS FROM HERE ON. WE IS LOSIN' MEN HAN'OVER FOOTS.
WHAT'D THAT CROWD OF ONE WANT IN THE FIRST PLACE?
WANTED TO TELL YOU I IS PASSED AWAY.

I DON'T SEE HOW WE COULD OF DWINDLED TO ONE WHEN THREE OF US IS LEFT.
BESIDES HOW DID THE RACKETY-COON-CHILE GIT COUNTED IN?

I FIGURE WE MUST OF FOUND THE CHILD! ACTUALLY, WE MUST ALL BE HEROES!
ALL ONE OF US?

RIGHT! EVERY MAN JACK OF US ONE!
PLOOOP!

Y'KNOW, YOU JUST CANT FOOL A HOUND'S SENSITIVE NOSE. I SMELL RAIN!
'TAINT THAT... THE TUB IS LEAKY.
OH, WELL, WE CAN'T GET VERY WET..... THEY ISN'T ANY OF US LEFT!

WHIRLED SERIES

YER OUT! I SAID STRIKE--- HE SAID STRIKE, --AN' THE CATCHER SAID STRIKE. THAT'S THREE! YER OUT!
THAT PITCH WAS OVER MY HEAD.

STOP COMPLAINING ABOUT BEING SHORT. THERE'S ONLY TWO STRIKES ON YOU---THE CATCHER'S CALL DOESN'T COUNT, ALBERT.
I'M POGO, NOT ALBERT!
I SAID STOP COMPLAINING AN' PLAY BALL!

STRIKE!
STRIKE?! WHY, THAT BALL HIT ME.

BELOW THE BELT?
RIGHT!
WHERE?
I WAS FACIN' SOUTH. SO IT WAS ON MY NORTH END!

HITTIN' BELOW THE BELT IS A FOUL---ANYBODY KNOW THAT---AN' A FOUL BALL IS A STRIKE--- SO, STRIKE SHE IS!
YOU IS GONNA GIT A NASTY LETTER FROM MY LAWYER IN THE MORNIN'!

STRIKE!
CAIRO

CAIRO

CAIRO

CAIRO

HOW'D YOU LIKE TO STEP OUTSIDE?
CAIRO

THERE'S A QUIET GROUND SWELL OF OPINION, DAZZLER, THAT YOUR PITCHIN' COULD BE DISPENSED WITH.
PHOO! IT'S THIS **JACK RABBIT** BALL--- BESIDES I ISN'T GITTIN' NO SUPPORT FROM YOU MENS.

NO **SUPPORT**? WE BRUNG BACK THE BALL FROM ALL 72 HOME RUNS.
YES, **BUT**, MR. MANAGER, SIR--- WHAT INNING IS IT?
VASSAR

FIRST HALF OF THE **FIRST** AND YOU ISN'T GOT **NO**BODY OUT YET!
HA! ***AND WHAT,*** PRAY TELL, IS THE SCORE?
THE UPSTATE RETURNS AREN'T IN SO FAR---BUT IT LOOKS LIKE 149 TO *NOTHIN'*.
SEE!? **SOME SUPPORT**---MY OWN TEAM ISN'T GOT ME **ONE MEASLE RUN** YET!
THE SUPERBAS
VASSAR II

I'LL PITCH FOR A WHILE---MAYBE I CAN PROTECT ***THEIR*** LEAD OF 149 TO NOTHIN' AND GET THE FIRST HALF OF THE FIRST INNING OVER----YOU PLAY LEFT FIELD.
INGRATE

I GOT IT! **I GOT IT! I GOT IT!**
CRACK

I GOT IT I GOT IT I GOT IT I GOT IT I GOT IT I G--

GAME'S OVER, POGO---WE LOST THE BALL.
I THOUGHT **HE** GOT IT!?
OH, HE **GOT** IT, ALLRIGHT!
'08

DON'T WRITE..
..DON'T WIRE!
SEE IF YOU CAN REVERSE CHARGES

WELL ... HERE WE ARE BACK AT THAT LETTER ... THAT AIRMAIL LETTER ...
NOW'S YOUR CHANCE TO TAKE TO THE WING ... WHO'S IT FOR?

THINK I'D BE A PAUL PRY TO READ THE ADDRESS?
IT SAYS "TO CHOO CHOO CURTIS, THE NATURAL BORN MAIL MAN."

WHY, IT'S FOR ME!
WHAT IS IT? WHATISITWHATIS ITWHATISITWHAT ISITWHATISIT?

OFFICIAL BUSINESS. MY WALKIN' PAPERS.
CONGRATULATIONS! NOW YOU DON'T HAVE TO FLY AN' CAN WALK TO DELIVER IT TO YOURSELF.
NOTICE OF DISMISSAL

BY JING! THE GUMMINT CAN'T FIRE ME!
BUT HERE IS THE OL' DISMISSAL NOTE.
OH HO! I HOLDS A TRUMP CARD. THE GUMMINT IS NEVER HIRED ME. I BEEN WORKIN' ON MY OWN. UN-BE-KNOWNS!
KEEPIN' IT A SECRET FROM 'EM? WHERE'S YO' GITS THE MAIL?

FELLER I KNOWS IS GOT A "IN." IT'S FIRST-CLASS STUFF HE GOT.
YOU REALIZE THIS MAKES YOU A SECRET AGENT FOR THE GUMMINT?
FIGGER THEY'LL SEND A CLUTCH OF SENATORS TO INVEST-IGATE ME?
IF THEY DOES, GIT A JOB WITH 'EM.. INVEST-IGATIN' YOU' OWN SELF ... YOU IS A EX-PERT ON YOU.

IF THE FEDERALS NEVER HIRED YOU AS A MAILMAN, HOW COULD THEY FIRE YOU?
THEY IS PERFECTED A SYSTEM.
I ISN'T FIRED AS A MAILMAN --- THEY FIRES ME OUT OF A JOB OF BEETLE ADMINISTRATOR.
BUT..
NOTICE OF DISMISSAL

YOU NEVER WAS A BEETLE ADMINISTRATOR.
THEY'S TOOKEN CARE OF THAT TOO. THIS LETTER SENT TO ME IS ACTUAL FOR THE COMMISSIONER OF TIDES IN TENNESSEE.
HARD FOR 'EM TO FIRE HIM OUTTA THE BEETLE JOB. YOU BETTER TELL THEM HE AIN'T YOU.
NO... IT WOULD ONLY CAUSE CONFUSION.

IF I UNNERSTANDS THIS RIGHTLY, THE FEDERALS DON'T KNOW YOU IS THE MAILMAN HERE-AN'-ABOUTS.
RIGHT!
BUT THEY WANTS TO FIRE YOU OUT OF THE BEETLE ADMINISTRATOR JOB WHICH YOU DON'T HAVE SO THEY SENDS YOU A LETTER FIRIN' THE COMMISSIONER OF TIDE FOR TENNESSEE?
RIGHT---AN I NEVER HEERD OF HIM.
SO...HE'S OUTEN A JOB?
YEP, BUT HE'LL NEVER KNOW IT--- THE LETTER WAS SENT IN 1946.
Y'KNOW, I THINK THIS IS ALL ON ACCOUNT OF YOU'S HANDLIN' SUCH A CHEAP BRAND OF MAIL NOWADAYS.
RIGHT! AN' IF I WOONT BE ACCUSED OF DISLOYALTY I'D START TAKIN' FROM ANOTHER JOBBER, BRAZIL, SAY. SERVE 'EM RIGHT TO START GITTIN' LETTERS IN PORTUGESE.
HEY, CHURCHY, HOW 'BOUT COMIN' UP THE HOUSE FO' SUPPER?
DOANMINEFFIEDOO, WILEY CATT.
I GOT A OL' COUSIN CRITTUR A-VISITIN' FROM UP KENTUCKAWAY.
CAT COUSIN, WILEY?

NOPE, A BIRD! HEY, THERE! I BRUNG HOME A TURTLE FOR SUPPER!

GOOD! I WAS WOND'RIN' WHAT WE'D HAVE.

PUT ON THE SKILLET NOW DON'T BE 'FRAID, MAMIE'S GONNA MAKE A LULA SHORTHAND BRAID
I DON'T LIKE THAT MENU YO' COUSIN IS MENTIONED AFORE.

DON'T CARE FOR SOUP?
BUT OL' COUSIN SAY HE GONE MAKE TURTLE SOUP.

HEY SARKY, COME OUT AN' MEET OL' TURTLE!
YOU SAID YOU HAD A TURTLE FO' SUPPER...

BUT I DIN'T KNOW THE COOK HAD TO BE INNERDUCED TO TH' INGREDIMINTS.
CHURCHY, MEET COUSIN SARCOPHAGUS MACABRE... UH, WHERE HE GO?

YESSIR, POGO, I GITS THE MAIL I DELIVERS FROM A BOY WHAT --- SAY-HERE COMES THAT BOY NOW!
WHOA, TURKLE!
IT'S OL' CHURCHY LA FEMME!

I WAS TELLIN' POGO HOW YOU WRITES ALL THE MAIL I DELIVERS 'ROUND THE SWAMP, SO COME ON OUT.

NO! I IS HIDIN' FROM A MAN BACK THAT WAY NAME OF SARCOPHAGUS MACABRE....WANTED ME TO GO INTO THE TURTLE SOUP BUSINESS WITH HIM---- HE FURNISHIN' THE POT AN' ME FURNISHIN' ME!
NO DEAL, HUH?

NOBODY'S AFTER YOU, COME ON OUT...
I DON'T WANT THAT BUZZARD TO FIND ME .... HE GOT A SWEET TOOTH FOR TURTLE SOUP!

SO YOU WRITES UP ALL THE MAIL WHAT OL' DUCK DELIVERS! YOU KNOW IT AIN'T REG'LAR U.S. AND A. TYPE OF MAIL.. MAYBE IT MEANS YOU IS BOOTLEGGIN' LETTERS.

GOSH.. IS IT AGIN THE LAW?
WELL.. UM—
HOWDY, GENTS, I'M FROM THE F.B.I. AN' I....
WHOOSH! LOOKY AT 'EM GO! HUMMPH, THIS JOB SELLIN' FOR THE FULSOME BRUSH INSTITUTE AIN'T GONNA BE NO BEDDA ROSES!

I'M SORRY WE RUN OUT ON YOU, MOUSE BUT WE'RE A MITE FRIGHTY.
YEH... I HEAR A BUZZARD HERE'BOUTS LIKES TURTLE SOUP.
HERE COMES SARCOPHAGUS MACABRE NOW!
JUST PULL YOUR HEAD INSIDE YOUR TRUNK COMPARTMENT, KIDDO.

STEP UP AN' SEE THE DANCIN' CLAM SHELL, NEIGHBOR.. A NICKEL IN THE SLOT AND HE JIGS AN' PRANCES! HURRY! HUR-REE!
GOOD THING HE WAS A LOVER OF THE ARTS... WE MADE 5..10..15... UH.. NO... ONE IS A BUTTON.
THAT'S MINE ...OFFA MY UNNERWEARS.

COUSIN SARCOPHAGUS MACABRE AN' ME IS HEERD THAT TURTLE IS BOOTLEGGIN' MAIL ... IT'S UNCONSTITUTABLE
AN' THAT'S A HANGIN' OFFENSE....! TREASON!
HANGIN'? TREASON? JES' 'CAUSE TURTLE'S BEEN A GOOD FELLA A-WRITIN' MAIL FER OL' DUCK TO DELIVER? HOW ELSE WOULD WE GIT LETTERS?

IT AIN'T THE FEDERAL WAY, SAM! JES' 'CAST A PEEPER OVER THIS REE-SIPPY FO' TURTLE SOUP.... DEE-LICIOWS!
RECIPES
TURTLE SOUP, MMM? Y'KNOW MAYBE THAT NO 'COUNT, UNDERHANDLED TURTLE IS DESTROYIN' OUR NATIONAL INSTITUTIONS... HANGIN' IS TOO GOOD FOR SUCH TRASH!
WELL, WE COULD HANG HIM A LI'L' BIT.

AH, THERE, DEACON MUSHRAT! KEEP A EYE OUT FOR OL' TURTLE! HE'S A MENACE!
For-sooth?
AYE ... HE'S DUE TO BE HUNG FER BOOTLEGGIN' MAIL! HE WRITES IT AN' THE DUCK DELIVERS IT.
Scandalum magnatum!
OOP!

AU CLAIR DE LA LUNE MON AMI PIER-ROT...
OH, SOLIO MELIO! RAZZ MAZZ MA TAZZ
A ORGAN GRINDER!
and his monkey!
WHAT'D HE MEAN? AND HIS MONKEY?
I DUNNO... BUT THE FOX PUT A SLUG IN THE HAT AN' THE DEACON LEFT A REQUEST, ...FOR US TO LEAVE FOR PARAGUAY...

Boy Bird Watchers Arise! Churchy Lafemme is a Dangerous menace! He must be watched, watched watched!
GOOD THING THERE'S THREE OF US.
SO US WILL SNOOP ON OL' TURTLE?
Snoop?! Goodness, what a horrid word! No, we'll make dignified intelligence reports.

IF HE'S A MENACE, US WILL BACK YOU TO THE LIMIT IF YOU WANTS TO FIGHT THE BOY.
US MAKE INTELLIGENCE REPORTS...? HAW!
Mercy, Fight?
It's not nice to fight, We merely report Turtle's Activies ~~~ others will handle him.
YOU COULD SEND HIM A POISON PEN LETTER.
UNDER SEPARATE COVER OF NIGHT.

TURTLE SAY US CAN SPY ON HIM 'LONG AS US DON'T GIT UNDER FOOTS.
H'LO BEAU-REGARD.
I NEEDS YOU TO WRITE SOMETHIN'.
..A FITTING SENTIMENT FOR ONE OF THE FINEST DOGS I EVER KNEW....
OKAY... HOW'S THIS?

"What gentler eye, What nobler heart doth warm the Winter day Than the true blue orb And the oaken core of our beloved old Dog Tray?"
GULP! GREAT--CHOKE--FITS TO A "T."
FOR A FRIEND, HUH? YOU WANT IT SENT?
GULK --SOB-- NO --- IT'S FOR ME. I'LL EAT IT HERE --- SNURF.

WATCHIN' THIS TURTLE BOOTLEG MAIL AIN'T THE SAME AS WATCHIN', SAY, LADY GODIVER.
HORSE OR NO HORSE, PEEKIN' IS PEIPING.
CAPITAL! COMMUNIST CAPITAL.
YOU KNOW THAT TURTLE WRITES A LOT OF THAT MAIL DOWN UNDER-BENEATH OF THE WATER?
I'M ABOUT TO SWEAR A MIGHTY BOY BIRD WATCHERS OATH--- HOW COME WE GOT THREE AN' A HALF ACES OF CLUBS?

AN' THAT PROVES HE MUST BE A MEMBER OF A UNDERWATER GROUP.
NATURALLY 'CAUSE HALF OF 'EM IS SPADES
HAUT GOÛT?
EN-GAGED IN SUBMERSIVE ACTIVITIES.
CAN'T BE SPADES, ALL FIVE ACES OF SPADES IS HERE ALREADIES.
YOU KNOW, WE MUST HAVE THE DEACON'S DECK... HE MARKS 'EM ILLITERATE

BEIN' A VIGILANTE COMMITTEE TO READ WHAT THE TURTLE WRITES IS HARD ON THE EYES, POGO.
WELL, READIN' IS A DANGEREST PRACTICE, SOMETIMES.
WRITIN' IS WORSE ...
LOOKY AT THAT LETTER I WROT IN SCHOOL.

I WROTE A EX-CUSE FOR BEWITCHED HERE AN' BOTHERED TELLS ME: MAKE THE TEACHER THINK WE IS GOT CLASS IN THE FAMBLY... SO.... 'STEAD OF SIGNIN' MY FATHER'S REAL NAME, LIKE A HONEST CHILE ----
I SIGNED: President Andrew Jackson --- WELL, SIR, WE WAS THROWED ALL THE WHOLE WAY TO ---
YOU SHOULD OF PICKED SOMEBODY ALIVE -- MEBBE OF ANOTHER PARTY.
THAT'S A TOUGH PARLAY.

I UNDERSTAND YOU BATS FIGGER TURTLE'S NOT SUCH A BAD FELLA ..... EVEN THOUGH HE BOOTLEGS MAIL!
WELL, IF IT ISN'T CHUCKLES!
LET ME READ YOU MEMBERS OF THE VIGILANTE COMMITTEE SOMETHING HE WROTE: "The Keen and the Quing Were quirling at quoits In the meadow behind of the mere.....

"Tho' mainly the meadow was middled with mow-- An heretical hitherto here!" THERE! DON'T THAT SOUND SNEAKY?
WELL, WE DON'T UNDERSTAND IT.
EXACTLY! IT'S THESE THINGS WE DON'T UNDERSTAND THAT ARE DANGEROUS!
GLAD YOU WARNED US... I DON'T UNDERSTAND YOU EITHER...
BY THE SAME TOKEN, I'M GOIN' OUT AN' SHOOT MY OLD GEOMETRY TEACHER

The Fox and others claim Turtle is a menace!
HE'S A TRAITOR
ALBERT, HOW COME YOU'RE AT A LADIES' AUXILIARY MEETING?
EATS. HOW COME YOU?

I'M REPORTER FOR A PAPER I MIGHT START. THESE CHARGES 'GAINST TURTLE IS SERIOUS.
WELL, I DON'T ALWAYS AGREE WITH TURTLE...
THEN YOU GOES ALONG WITH OL' FOX AN' CAT AN' SARCOPHAGUS MACABRE?
COURSE NOT... IF I CAN'T AGREE WITH MY FRIENDS, HOW YOU 'SPECT ME TO G'T 'LONG WITH MY ENEMIES?

To prove Turtle has been bootlegging Mail, let me present Dr. Kidney of the Kidney-Garden Researches, who is an expert on the Sectional Problems of the American Mails-- He has a word 'bout Turtle.
GUILTY.

PSST---OWL, IF YOU GITS A CHANCE, SLIP CHURCHY A LI'L' SUMPIN'...I BRUNG HIM IN THE BAG 'CAUSE HE WASN'T INVITED FORMAL...
YU HU
DOESN'T YOU KNOW THIS IS A PROTEST MEETIN' 'GAINST YOU?
YEP, AN' I FEELS I IS SWIPIN' THESE RATIONS UNDER FALSE PRETENSES 'COZ I IS FOR ME.
(MY CONSCIENCE HURT ME)

WELL, IF IT ISN'T MY COUSINS, THE BATS! NOTHIN' LIKE A LI'L' SATURDAY GAME.
WHAT'S YOU HEAR 'BOUT OL' TURTLE?
SIT IN! SIT IN!

I'LL DEAL THE CARDS OVER AGAIN.
DON'T BOTHER, I BRUNG A PACK OF MY OWN ····· THEY'RE GONNA SPRING A SPY QUEEN ON TURTLE.

IT'S HARD FANNIN' 52 ... BUT, WHAT YOU PLAYIN', FRIENDS? ···THIS SPY QUEEN SET UP REMINDS ME OF ONE TIME I'M UP IN D.C. AND ····
I GOT A GOOD PINOCHLE HAND... HE'S PLAYIN' WHIST AN' BEWITCHED IS A POKER MAN.
THEY HAUL ME IN AN' SAY "WAS YOU EVER IN CAHOOTS WITH A LOVELY SPY QUEEN" AN' I SAY "NO, BUT I SPENT A SEASON IN RANGOON WITH A LADY BASEBALL TEAM..."
SAY, THIS IS A OLD MAID DECK I GOT ···
AW.. GO AHEAD LEAD!

"Ladies of the Vigilante Auxiliary, here's a book written by a loyal lady spy = "I was an ex-member of the Underground." -- The material on Turtle ~
I WAS AN EX-MEMBER OF THE UNDERGROUND

~ is so secret, that the book had to be composed entirely of Blank paper.
BY TARNAL FIRE, IF HE AIN'T RIGHT!

Now who is the beautiful spy queen who watched Turtle's submersive work? None other than ~~~~~~~~~
Lucy! Lucy, the beautiful jelly fish, brought here in a jelly jar ---- wait 'til we take the lid off this!
A REAL SIGH-REEN!
It's hard to get the top off the jelly jar so's Lucy, the jelly-fish, can tell 'bout bein' a Beautiful Spy Queen --
soon's we get her outen there ----- we'll -- oop -- she's slippery ---
SHE BROKE.
can this be Lucy? Looks like she's real jelly --
BIG PIECES OF RASPBERRY ALL OVER
MFF.. MOULDY!
Where'd you get that Spy Queen?
LEFT OVER FROM A PARTY.
Y'AINT S'POSE TO OPEN UP EVERYTHIN IN PUBLIC.

Finally we have a cryptic bit written by Turtle that reeks of guilt.
"SMILE, WAVERING WINGS, ABOVE RAIN'S POUR, WHILE HOPEFULLY SINGS LOVE OF SHORN SHORE. SHORE SHORN OF LOVE SINGS HOPEFULLY WHILE, POUR RAINS ABOVE, WINGS WAVERING, SMILE."
I DON'T GIT IT.
THAT'S THE CLEVER PART. IT'S GOTTA BE READ BACKWARD.
YEP! IT GOES FROM RIGHT TO LEFT.
Here it is backward: "Smile, wavering wings, Above rain's pour, While hopefully sings Love of shorn shore. Shore shorn of Love Sings hopefully while pour rains above Wings wavering smile."
THERE!
YOU KNOW, IF I DIN'T HEAR YOU READ THAT, I WOULDN'T BELIEVE MY EARS!
WELL, IT LOOKS LIKE THE EVIDENCE IS PILED UP AGIN TURTLE...
ONLY THING EVIDENT SO FAR IS THE FOX, CAT AN' BUZZARD WANTS HIM IN THE SOUP.
BUT YOU SAW THE SPY BOOK!
FULL OF BLANK PAPER!

THAT'S BECAUSE EVERYTHING IN IT WAS HUSH-HUSH! AN' THAT POEM HE WROTE---WHOOIE! YOU CAN'T DENY THAT?!
DENY IT? IT'S JUST A NONSENSE VERSE .... FORWARD OR BACK-WARD!
WELL, YOU GOTTA ADMIT IT'S A DEVIOUS WRITER WHAT CAN MEAN NOTHING IN TWO DIRECTIONS AT THE SAME TIME.
EVER'BODY DECIDE TO HANG TURTLE?
I'M GONNA MAKE UP THEIR MINDS FOR 'EM ---A HUNG TURTLE OUT-RANKS A HUNG JURY.
AN ACT OF KIND-NESS ---SPARIN' TURTLE THAT WORRY...
DEACON! YOU FIND OL' TURTLE YET?
The others say they're havin' trouble findin' Turtle guilty ---- but I can't find him nohow -- Guilty or Innocent. I better beat a dignified retreat.
HAND ME THAT OL' MUSHRAT RECIPE!

Let me in -- them varmints is out to git me 'cause I didn't deliver the Turtle into their hands ---
THERE'S CAVE ENOUGH FOR ONE MORE.
Finally I said, "This is an innocent man you're tryin' to frame --" and They said, "Always remember the next innocent man might be you!"

YOU AN INNOCENT MAN?! WHAT A BASE CANARD!
AN OUTRAGE!
YOU SHOULD OF PUNCHED HIM RIGHT IN THE EYE.
I'll have you know I can be innocent as the next man!
DEPENDS ON WHO YOU'RE NEXT TO.
THEY'D NEVER CATCH ME BEIN' INNOCENT.
NOT THESE DAYS.

MY, DON'T YOU THINK IT'S COURAGEOUS OF THE DEACON AN' ALL TO PROVE OL' TURTLE'S GUILTY?
WHAT DID THEY FINALLY PROVE HIM GUILTY OF, HON?
NUTS
OH, HEE HEE! LAND, SUGAR, I BEEN SO BUSY I NEVER DID PAY THAT PART NO MIND.
THOSE AS KNOW WAS SURE HE'S GUILTY OF WHAT-EVER IT WAS, HOWEVER.
WHERE THEY'S SMOKE THEY'S FIRE, HON.

EVER'BODY'S WORD 'GAINST HIS'N. ----- FACT IS, HE NEVER SAID NOTHIN'.
NOW THEY'S OUT AFTER HIM ---- WELL, 'TAINT MY AFFAIR- I MIND MY OWN BUSINESS AN' STAY COMFY..

AN' OUT OF TROUBLE.
NUTS, HON?
WK

SEED A TURTLE, STRANGER?
WELL, IF IT ISN'T LAUGHING GAS.

WHO'S YOU TO COME GAR-BARGIN' IN CALLIN' ME STRANGER?! YOU IS STRANGER NOR ME.

WHAT'S IN THE BASKET?
THAT THERE BASKET THERE? WHY, TURTLE'S INSIDE HIDIN' FROM YOU.
VERY FUNNY----DO YOU TAKE ME FOR A FOOL?
I WOULDN'T TAKE YOU FOR NOTHIN'!

Let me hide in there too, Churchy? Them varmints is after me, too!
HELP YO'SELF, DEACON, I GOIN' OUT FOR A BATH.
I HEAR TELL TURTLE IS IN THAT BASKET OF ALBERT'S.
FINE--- I KNOW WHERE IT IS--- COME ON.

'SPOSE HE IS IN THAT BASKET?
No, he isn't! Go away!

HA! NOW WE GOT HIM! DON'T SLIP ON THESE STONES!

WHILE I WAS SLEEPIN' SOMEBODY STOLE TURTLE IN MY LUNCH BASKET---
I SAW 'EM! IT WAS THAT OL' BUZZARD, NAME OF SARCOPHAGUS MACABRE, AN' OL' WILEY CATT.
THEY CAN'T STEAL YOU FROM UNDER MY NOSE THAT WAY!

BUT ISN'T I HERE? YEP! IT'S ME... SEE MY NAME'S ON THIS TOWEL I IS USIN'.
GOOD! I WAS 'BOUT TO REVENGE YO' DEE-MISE.
CHURCHY
BE NICE IF YOU RESCUE DEACON! IT WAS HIM THEY SWUP IN YO' BASKET.
DUNNO 'BOUT THAT; BUT TWO INNOCENT EGG SAN'WICHES WAS IN THERE, TOO!

THEY'S UP THERE GITTIN' READY TO COOK OL' DEACON!
YOU FIGGER US IS GONE BE TOO LATE?

OH, I FIGGER THEY'LL BE SOME LEFT, THO' THEY VERY LIKELY AIN'T GONNA SAVE US ANY....

OPEN UP THERE!
GO AWAY!

WHEN NEIGHBORS COME CALLIN', ACK POLITE!

NOW, YOU CANNIBOBBLES! I IS COMED FOR MY LUNCH WHAT YOU STOLED AND INCIDENTLY FOR DEACON, TOO.
I AIN'T FEARED OF YO' GUN! YOU'LL TAKE DEACON OVER HIS DEAD BODY!
WAIT

RUN, RUN! OUR SATURDAY NIGHT BATH AIN'T DUE 'TIL APRIL — AN' THAT BOY IS SPORTIN' A WATER PISTOL.
WHY, SO I IS.
HALP!
GANG-WAYS!
PLOOP
PLOOP

Oh, how can I ever thank you for rescuing me from them frightful people...
DON'T YOU BITE!
SMACK
LONG AS THE LUNCH IS GONE, US MOUGHT'S WELL HEAD BACK.
You dear courageous handsome an' brave hero— Let me help you carry your ...

IF YOU DON'T STOP BEIN' GRATEFUL I IS GONE POP YOU!
HEY, THERE! IS WE TOO LATE TO RESCUE TH' DEACON?
NO! ACTUAL YOU IS JUST IN TIME TO RESCUE HIM FROM HIS RESCUERS.
?

ALL THAT INVESTIGATION INTO CHURCHY'S LIFE BY DEACON WASTED... MY MY!
I DUNNO 'BOUT THAT .... WE SURE LEARNED A LOT 'BOUT OL' DEAC'!
IT'S A-ONE AN' A-TWO AN' A SEE-LIDE, BOY!
YEP ... IT DON'T PAY TO INVESTIGATE TOO MUCH ... A BOY FALLS OVERBOARD WEIGHED DOWN WITH NOTES AN' HE'S REAL GONE!
OH, HE'S DEEP!

IGNORANCE IS A BANE, MY FRIENDS.... NOW, AS FOR ME, I GOT KNOWLEDGE WHAT I HARDLY AIN'T TOUCHED YET.
SOON AS THE PLAYIN' FIELDS ARE CLEAR OF ICE LET'S CHOOSE UP SIDES .... WE CAN HANDLE OUR IGNORANCE, CAN YOU HANDLE YOUR LINE OF
IT'S A-ONE AND A RUFFLE AND A BUFFLE AND A BUFFLE O'SHUFFLE

MAGNA CUM LHUDE SING CUCCU

SH! DOCTOR OWL IS EX-AMININ' OUR NEW MECHANIWOCKLE MAN...
GOOD SOUND PULSE
WHAT YOU SHOOSHIN' ME FOR--I GOTS MUCH RIGHT IN THIS STRIP AS
IN MY CONSIDER OPINIONS I FEEL

RRING RING RINGY RING RING
HELLO? DOC OWL'S OFFICE... DOC IS TEMPORARY UN-DISPOSE.
HELLO? WHAT? HE IS?

WHAT GOOD IS THIS HUMAN BEAN YOU INVENTED?
IT SOLVES PROBLEMS. WATCH IT ADD ONE AN' ONE.

RING GG
RING RR
RING

THERE!
FOOF! I CAN ADD BETTERN THAT.
YOU GOTTA REMEMBER, THIS MACHINE IS MERE A HUMAN BEAN---
IT'S NOT LIKE IT WAS A MECHANICAL DOG OR OTHER KIND OF BEAST... GIVE IT A CHANCE.
YEAH, FAIR IS FAIR, YOU KNOW.

WHAT'S ALL THIS FUSS 'BOUT POLITICS, MR. TAM-MANANNY? IS IT WHAT BRINGS YOU BACK TO THE SWAMP?
CONFIDENTIAL SPEAKIN'--YES. I'M AN EMISARRY FROM THE OLD MAIN GUARD..
THE PARTY BIG-WIGS BRIEFED ME ON WHAT THEY EXPECT OF THE BIG BOY... WHAT THEY THINK THE BIG BOY'S POLICIES OUGHT TO BE---SO I'M GONNA ASK HIM IF HE WANTS TO RUN.

WHO IS THIS BIG BOY?
WHO? HA! WHAT A QUESTION--- WHO, INDEED..

BY GOLDERN! I KNEW THERE WAS SOME LI'L' THING I FERGOT TO FIND OUT.

MR. TAMMANANNY WAS SENT 'ROUND BY POLITICOS TO SOUND OUT THE BIG BOY.
CAN'T RECALL WHO HE IS.... BUT A CANDIDATE FOR THE TOP JOB GOTTA BE SMART, HONEST AND A FEARLESS LEADER.
I WAS CUT IN ON ALL THAT STUFF AN' IS YOU NOTICED WHAT A BIG ONE I IS?
OOG! BUT WAS YOU BORN IN A LOG CABIN?

YOU MEAN A BIG TYPE OF FEARLESS LEADER LIKE ME GOTTA BE BORNED IN A BACKWOODS HUT?
OH, MY DEAR SIR, IT'S A ABSOLUTE IRREDEEMABLE VIRTUE --(IE: CAN'T DO WITHOUT IT.)
BY NAB! YOU HEAR THAT? MY MAM AN' PAP IS SWUNDLED ME OUTEN THE PRESIDENSITY OF THE NATURAL BORN COUNTRY!
IT WAS CLOSE THOUGH -- MIGHTY CLOSE, FRIENDS.

HOW YOU LIKE THAT? OL' TIGER SAY A MAN GOTTA BE BORN IN A LOG CABIN TO BE PRESIDENT OR ELSE...
ELSE... ?
ELSE HE SAY THE MAN GOTTA HAVE A POWERFUL MACHINE BEHINE OF HIM --- HUNNERDS OF VOTERS AN' ......
MACHINE?

ALBERT! THAT MECHANIWOCKLE MAN WE INVENTED! YOU REALIZE WHAT IT REALLY IS?
A LADY?
IT'S THE START OF OUR OWN MACHINE! WE'LL MAKE THOUS-ANDS OF THEM LI'L' FELLERS AN' PUT 'EM ALL OUT TO VOTIN' ROUN' THE CLOCK... A TWENTY-FOUR HOUR DAY.
MAYBE EVEN A TWENNY FIVE HOUR DAY.
POGO, HAND OVER YO' CLOCK. I IS GONE MAKE A HUMAN BEAN OUTEN IT SO'S IT CAN VOTE FOR ME.
IT'S NOT OLD ENOUGH TO VOTE.
IT LOOKS OLD ENOUGH.
THAT'S JES' 'CAUSE ITS RUN DOWN A LI'L'.
YEOW! A LI'L' ANIMAL TYPE VARMINT!
NO, IT'S A BIRD... HARMLESS NOR A CATER-PIGGLE.
CUCKOO CUCK-KOOHOO
LEMME AT IT... I'LL TEACH IT TO POP OUT AT INNOCENT PEOPLE.
IS THAT ANY WAY TO TREAT YOUR CONSTITUENCY?

MAM HEERD TELL A MAN OVER HERE FIGGERS HE'S GONE RUN FOR PUBLIC OFFICE..
RIGHT THIS WAY, SIR.
MAM SENT THE TADS OVER TO BE KISSED UP. US CAN'T BEAR KISSIN' THE UGLY LI'L' SPRATS OURSELFS BUT WE UNDERSTAN'S YOU POLITICIANS KISSES 'EM FREE OF CHARGE.
HERE'S THE FIRST YOUNG 'UN.. BOY GO BY NAME OF MERMSY.
MERMSY?
HE'S A WAITIN' ON YOU.
PUCKER UP, MERM! AND STOP YO' BELLERIN'.
DO I GOTTA DO THIS?
A PUBLIC OFFICE IS A PUBLIC TRUST.
THE SCENE SHIFTS (UNEASILY)
WHAT'S THE BRAIN TRUST UP TO?
THEY'S MAKIN' A MECHANIWOCKLE MAN SO'S IT'LL VOTE FOR THEM IF THEY RUNS FOR ANYTHING.
MMPH - STBBT GRSR - YEEP
-- RUNS FOR ANY-THIN'? YOU MEAN LIKE THE BORDER?
YOU BLAGSTAGGY LI'L' BLAGGARD! HOLE TO-GETHER!

OH... I WAS CARRIED AWAY! IT'S RUINT... I FEEL LIKE I MURDERED MY OWN CHILE .... HOW WILL I EVER ANSWER TO MY CONSCIENCE?

YOU COULD PLEAD INSANITY.
AN' WE'D BACK YOU UP.
PHOO! AIN'T EITHER OF YOU GOT NO SENTIMINTS?

OWL, IF YOU AN' ALBERT IS BUILDIN' A MACHINE CANDIDATE, YOU CAN USE THIS OL' GRAN'DADDY CLOCK OF MINE.
DANDY! JES' JAMES DANDY.

CUCKOO! CUCKOO! FOUR-SEVENTY-FIVE AND ALL IS WELL!
WHOO! HE DON'T EVEN KNOW WHAT TIME IT IS.

IT'S SATURDAY, BRIGHT EYES! WANNA MAKE SOMETHIN' OUT OF IT?!
YES. MAKE IT WEDNESDAY AND I'LL SETTLE FOR THAT FOUR SEVENTY-FIVE.

WHO'S THE AUTHORITARY ON THIS STUFF? ME OR THAT GOOGLYMUSH?
I DUNNO, POGO, YOU THINK I CAN MAKE A CANDIDATE OUTEN A CLOCK WHAT GOT A RABBIT FOR A CUCKOO?
WHY NOT?

THINK THIS OUGHT TO HAVE A MUSTACHE LIKE GROVER?
OWL IS BUILDIN' A MACHINE CANDIDATE.
HOW FEARSOMELY DROLL.
EIGHTY-FOUR O'CLOCK! CUCKOO-HOO! WEATHER FORECAST: RAIN AND..

CAN'T YOU CONTAIN YOURSELF 'TIL EASTER? YOU'RE ONLY SPOSED TO STRIKE ON THE HOUR.
FOOF!
BY JING, IF YOU GET FANCY WITH ME, I'LL STRIKE EVERY FIFTEEN MINUTES AN' I'LL PULL OUT EVERY CUCKOO 'TWEEN HERE AN' CAP-ITOL HILL.
DON'T ROUSE ORGANIZED TYPES.

IT EVER OCCUR TO YOU THAT THIS CLOCK IS ORGANIZED? YOU THROW ME OUT AN' THERE WON'T BE ANOTHER TICK OUTEN THIS OUTFIT......
DOG BONE! THEN YOU CAN HAVE THE WHOLE WORKS! I QUIT AS OWNER!
HEY! YOU'RE UNFAIR TO THE HELP! YOU CAN'T GIVE ME THE BUSINESS! HOW'LL I STRIKE?
EASY! JUST AS INACCURATE AS EVER!

HOW COME YOU IS PICKETIN' THE GRAND OL' DADDY CLOCK, BUN RABBIT?
UNFARE

OWL GOT TIRED OF IT AN' GIVE IT AT ME AN', SINCE I IS THE RESIDENT CUCKOO, I IS STRIKIN' FOR A FIFTEEN MINUTE HOUR.
WANT SHORTER HOURS?

AN' LOWER RENTS FOR ME, THE TENANT.
BUT YOU IS LAN'LORD, TOO. WHY DON'T YOU NEGOTIATE?
UNFARE

THE LAN'LORD IS MAD AT THE TENANT AN' ISN'T SPEAKIN' TO MYSELF AN' EVEN IF THEY WAS, THE NEIGHBORS WOULD THINK I HAD TOOK LEAVE OF OUR SENSES.
TRUE... TRUE.... TEE-ROO.

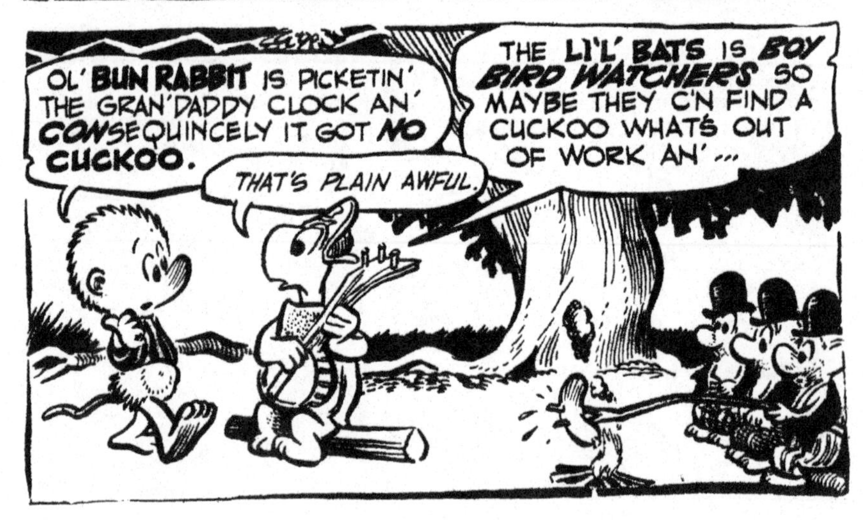
OL' BUN RABBIT IS PICKETIN' THE GRAN'DADDY CLOCK AN' CONSEQUINCELY IT GOT NO CUCKOO.
THAT'S PLAIN AWFUL.
THE LI'L' BATS IS BOY BIRD WATCHERS SO MAYBE THEY C'N FIND A CUCKOO WHAT'S OUT OF WORK AN'...

WHAT!? YOU ASK US TO BREAK THE LAW?
BIRD WATCHIN' DON'T START 'TIL SPRING... YOU WANT US TO GO TO JAIL FER WATCHIN' 'EM OUT OF SEASON?

I IS GONE HAFTA LOOK FOR A CUCKOO BIRD MYSELF; WON'T YOU LI'L' BATS HELP?
YOU ASK US TO SULLY OUR BIRD WATCHERS' OATH BY WATCH-ING BIRDS OUTTA SEASON?
OH, WELL.
YOU WOULDN'T WANT US TO JEE-OPPARDIZE OUR PRISTINE POSITION WITH THE NATIONABLE SO-CIETY?

IT'S TOO MUCH TO EXPECT US UNSPOILT LI'L' FELLAS TO....
OKAY! O-KAY! YOU'RE PURE! YOU'RE PURE! I JUST THOUGHT IT MIGHT BE REWARDING TO....
REWARDING? WELL, NOW SIR! WELL-WELL-WELL!
HOW MUCH?

THE LI'L' BATS AN' ME IS ALL OUT LOOKIN' FOR A CUCKOO BIRD.
A COOCOO, HUH.
HON. ANDY LYON

Sumer is icumen in,
Lhude sing cuccu ---
Groweth sed
an' bloweth med
An' springth the wude nu,
Sing cuccu!
SHOOSH

Cuccu, cuccu, wel
Singes thu, cuccu,
Na swike thu naver nu;
Sing cuccu, nu ---
Sing cuccu,
Sing cuccu,
Sing cuccu!

WE GOT US ONE!
cu?

WHO YOU?
COCCYZUS ERYTHROPHTHALMUS. A NATURAL BORN CUCKOO BY TRADE. I HEAR YOU BOYS GOT A JOB FOR ME.

YEP, YOU GOTTA GET IN A CLOCK AN' HOLLER OUT THE HOURS ....
MY HOLLER GO: GOWK! KULK! KOW-WUK! MOURNFUL IT IS.
YOU AIN'T FOOLIN'
CAP'N DAN'S

CAPTAIN DAN, THE OGLIN' MAN, SAY YOU BIRDS EATS QUANTITIES OF FUZZY TENT CATER-PIGGLES.
NO WONDER YOU GO "GOWK."
IT'S THE A-MERICAN WAY.
CAP'N DAN'S ATLAS

ONLY THE EUROPEAN CUCKOO SAYS "CUCKOO." ?
I JES' HOPE I NEVER HEARS YOU STRIKE MIDNIGHT! --MORE'N A HALF DOZEN OF THEM GOWKS AN' KOW-WUKS WOULD GIVE ME THE QUANDARIES.

EVEN IF YOU DON'T SAY: "COO-COO" GOOD, WHY NOT TAKE THE CLOCK JOB, ANYWAYS?
IT'S A NICE PUBLIC OFFICE. AN' YOU ONLY HAFTA COUNT UP TO TWELVE.
COR!

AN' EVERY HOUR ON THE HOUR, IT'S OUTSIDE WORK.
BUT US AMERICAN CUCKOOS GOES "KOW-WUK."

HIRE A EUROPEAN CUCKOO. THEM KIND GOES "COO-COO" VERY NICELY.
IS YOU IMPLYIN' THAT A RED-BLOODED A-MERICAN ISN'T THE CUCKOO THAT A EUROPEAN IS?

IT'S A ORNITHO-LOGICAL FACT.
I QUESTION THIS BIRD'S LOYALTY. HE COULD AT LEAST SPEAK AMERICAN.

AND, AFTER 16 HOURS OF PRACTICING

AS A FAVOR, I'LL PAINT THESE NUMBERS ON YO' STOMACH, TURTLE.
THANKS
US WANTS TO SET OUR NEW CLOCK, WHAT TIME YOU GOT?
NONE TO SPARE.
IF THE CLOCK IS ANY GOOD IT OUGHT TO HAVE TIME OF ITS OWN.

COO-COO! COO-COO! TWO O'CLOCK!
YUMP!
IF TIME-TELLIN' IS COMIN' TO THAT, I IS SWEARIN' OFF! THIS OL' WATCH IS HAD FIVE O'CLOCK ON HER SINCE 1936 AN' UP TO NOW I NEVER DOUBTED IT.

THERE'S BUN RABBIT STILL PICKETIN' HIMSELF 'CAUSE HE'S A TENANT IN THE CLOCK OF WHICH HE IS ALSO THE LAN'LORD.
UNFAIR

ENEMY OF THE LITTLE PEOPLE! OPPRESSOR OF THE POOR! BAH!

SEEIN' AS YOU IS THE LANDLORD OF THE CLOCK US GOT A NEW CLOCKWORKS FOR YOU, SIR.
I'M ALSO THE TENANT AN' IS PICKETIN' THE GOUGIN' CAPITALISTIC LAN'LORD.
JUST BE THE LANDLORD FOR A MINUTE WHILST US PUTS IN THE WORKS.
MMM... MOUGHT AS WELL........ HERE, HOLE THIS A LI'L' MINUTE.
UNFARE

NOW I'M THE LAN'LORD AN'... HEY! IS YOU PICKETIN' THIS ESTABLISHMINT?
NO, I..
BEGONE CHURL! OFF WITH YOUR PARA-SITICAL PROLETARIAN VULGARITIES! A POX ON YOU! FIE!
UNFAIR
FIE?

WHAT'S YOU PICKETIN' ME FOR, POGO?
IT'S YOUR SIGN! ALL I'M DOIN' IS HOLDIN' IT FOR YOU.
UNF-ARE
A LIKELY STORY! YOU'VE THROWED A PICKET LINE UP SOS I CAN'T GIT A NEW CUCKOO FER MY CLOCK.

BUT YOU ASKED ME TO.... YOU WAS A TENANT PICKETIN' YOU, THE LANDLORD, AN' YO' SAY "HOLE THIS!" I'M GONE APPEAL TO THE RENT CONTROL OFFICER.

WON'T DO NO GOOD. I'M THE RENT CONTROL OFFICER, TOO. NEITHER THE TENANT NOR THE LANDLORD TRUSTS ME!
YOU IS PREJUDICED AGAINST RABBITS.
IS YOU SURE THEY NEEDS A CUCKOO?

I'D LEAVE THIS GRAN'FATHER CLOCK TO ITS OWN MISER'BLE DEE-VICES IF I COULD JUST GIT AWAY.

WHY CAN'T YOU? GO AHEAD, LEAVE.
I CAN'T LOCK UP. CAN'T FIND THE KEY.

WHY YOU GOTTA LOCK UP? IS THEY SOMETHIN' VALUABLE IN THERE?
YEP! THEY IS A VERY IMPORTANT ITEM IN THERE SOMEPLACE. DON'T WANT NOBODY TO GIT IT, SO I GOTTA LOCK IT UP.

WHAT IN THE EVER-BE LOVIN' WORLD IS IT?
THE KEY.... THE KEY WHAT I CAN'T FIND! THE KEY TO LOCK IT UP IS WHAT'S IN THERE.

IS YOU SERIOUS WHEN YOU SAYS YOU WANTS TO LOCK UP THE CLOCK TO SAFEGUARD SOMETHIN' IN THERE AN' THE SOMETHIN' IN THERE IS THE KEY?
YEP, AN' I CAN'T FIND IT---- IT'S VERY UNBARRASS-ING.
I GOT A VERY CLEVER SUGGESTION.
TAKE OFF YO' HAT WHEN YOU ADDRESS A LADY.
I AIN'T NO HAT.

WE IS EVEN UP. I ISN'T NO LADY.
WHY NOT SET FIRE TO THE CLOCK AN' SIFT THE ASHES AN' FIND THE KEY EASY?
GREAT! THEN WE CAN FIND TH' LOCK-----
AN' LOCK IN THE KEY ALL SAFE!
LET'S GO OVER TO MY HOUSE AN' HAVE MILK AN' COOKIES AN' FERGIT THESE PANELS

IF WE SETS FIRE TO THE CLOCK TO FIND THE KEY IN THE ASHES, HOW'LL WE PUT IT OUT?
I'LL HOLLER: FIRE!

WHERE?

NO-WHERES YET! WHAT'S YOU DOIN' IN OUR CLOCK?
IT WAS EMPTY SO I USIN' IT FOR A FIREHOUSE.... YOU TURNED IN A FALSE ALARM!
AN' THAT'S A PENAL O-FFENSE ... BUT I'LL KEEP YOU OUT OF TROUBLE BY SETTIN' ONE OF YOU ON FIRE AN'....
EVER'BODY IS NICE TO US....
IT'S JES' 'CAUSE WE IS SO CUDDABLE.

AS I WAS SAYIN', LONG AS YOU TURNED IN A FALSE ALARM - I CAN SET FIRE TO ONE OF YOU TO KEEP YOU OUT OF TROUBLE.
S'POSE I IS CONFLAGRATED, GIMME A DEMONSTRATION OF HOW YOU GONE PUT ME OUT? I WANTS THE BEST.
IF YOU WANTS THE BEST, I GIVES YOU THE TWO DOLLAR JOB.... FIRST WE SOAKS THE HOLOCAUST WITH GOOD WET WATER..
VERY NICE.
WITH THE INFERNO MO-MENTARY CHECKED, THE BRAVE SMOKE-EATER CHOPS A HOLE IN THE ..... HEY! HOLD STILL!
YEAH.. BE A SPORT.
I GOTTA GO HOME AN' TAKE MY ASBESTOS PILLS.

PEACE OF CHANGE

THAT LI'L' CLOCKWORK HUMAN BEAN I MADE IS RUN OFF.
JES' LIKE THE GINGERBREAD BOY EXCEPT NOT SO APPETIZING.

HAVE A CARE HOW YOU SPEAKS! THAT WAS MY OWN FLESH AN' BLOOD
HE WAS YOUR SPITTIN' IMAGE TOO. UNCOUTH AN' INCONDITE.

HOW DOUBLE-DARE DAST YOU SPEAK TO A BEREAVED DADDY-BOY LIKE THAT?
GOK

BESIDES USIN' INSULTIN' WORDS WHAT I DON'T UNDER-STAND, YOU FIGHTS DIRTY! YOU BIT ME ON THE SEEGAR.

THE LI'L' HUMAN BEAN IS RUNNED AWAY FROM HOME.
STOP **BLUBBERIN'!** IT WAS ONLY MADE OF A **CLOCK** AN' **STICKS.**
WE SHOULD NEVER OF LEFT **CARLSBAD!** ***WHAT HATH THITH SWAMP WROUGHT NOW?***

TICK
TICK! TICK TICK
TICK TICK TICK!
TICK! TICK!
TICK TICK TICK
TEE-HICK
TICK
TINK

YOU HAD OUGHT TO DO **SOME-THIN'** FER THEM **HICCUPS**, JACK. **LIKE PUTTIN' OVER THE HEAD A BAG** OR MEBBE A DRINK OF WATER...?
*OR WE CAN GIVE HIM A **GOOD** SCARE.*
WHAT FOR A **GOOD** ONE? HE MERE GAVE ***US*** A **BAD** ONE.

LET'S TAKE THIS LI'L' ***HIC-CUPPIN' CRITTUR*** OVER TO **POGO** AN' SEE WHAT HE CALLS IT.
TICK TICK TICK TICK!
TICK TICK TICK

TAKE OFF YOUR HAT WHEN YOU GOES IN.
POGO

RING RING RING RINGY RINGY RING RING RING
DOOR BELL! DOOR BELL! I'LL GIT IT. I'LL GIT IT.
HELLO? HALLOO? SOMEBODY RING???? THAT'S FUNNY.... NOBODY'S THERE.
TICK TICK?

AS LONG AS POGO'S NOT HOME LET'S DIVIDE UP HIS COOKIES 'TIL HE GITS BACK AN' TEACH THE MECHANICAL CRITTUR A GENTEEL GAME OF SKILL.
HOO BOY!
HEE HEE

HEY, YOU'RE NOT S'POSED TO LEAVE YOUR CARDS FACE UP!
NOW, DON'T INNERFERE WITH THE STRANGER'S STYLE, FRIEND.
LACY FAIR, BOYS, LAY-SEE FAIR!

HMM.... HE SEEM TO BE EMPLOYIN' A DOUBLE WING WITH LIMITLESS SUBSTITUTIONS.
US BETTER FALL BACK AN' REE-GROUP.
IT MIGHT RAIN BEFORE THE FIFTH INNING.

WELL, ONCE AGAIN IT'S PROVEN THAT NINE KINGS BEATS SIX OF A KIND.
WHAT'S HE WANT WITH OUR PANTS THOUGH?
MEBBE HE KNOWS A NAKED OCTOPOTS

YOUR FINE FEATHERED FRIEND, ALBERT, MADE A HUMAN BEAN TYPE OF BURGLAR WHAT IS LAYIN' WASTE OUR FAIR SWAMP.
LAYIN' WASTE? WHAT'S YOU MEAN?
HE SWUPPED OUR PANTS!
HIC HIC
THERE THERE.

LI'L' BEWITCHED IS SO UPSET THAT HE GITS HICCUPS AN' US HAS TO JOG HIM.
HIC HIC HIC HIC HIC HIC
WHY'S IT UPSET YOU SO MUCH?
HOW'D YOU LIKE TO STAND AROUN' WITH NO PANTS? WHAT WOULD YOU DO?
HIC HIC HIC
HIC?

THERE HE IS... CAREFREE AN' GAY. LITTLE CARIN' IF HE MADE US LOSE OUR PANTS...
NEVER DO HE KNOW WHAT'S THE GAME...
NOR WHOM IS PLAYIN' WHOM.
4-1

IF THE SCORE IS OVER 2-0, HE AIN'T GONE COUNT IT.
YEH, HE DOES ALL HIS FIGGERIN' ON HIS FINGER-BONES.
BUT DON'T HE GOT A NORMAL NUMBER?
WELL -- NORMAL AS ALLIGATORS GO; BUT WHEN HE GITS THINKIN' WITH HIS FINGERS, HE'S ALL THUMBS.

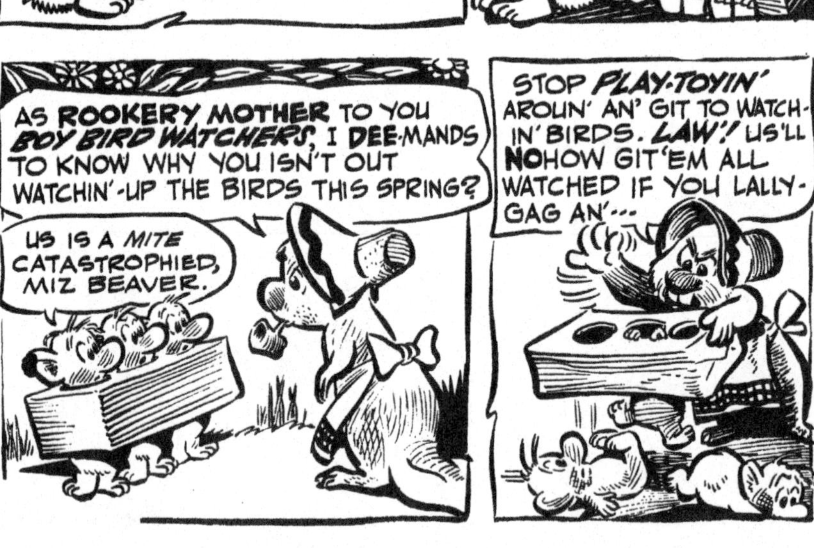
AS ROOKERY MOTHER TO YOU BOY BIRD WATCHERS, I DEE-MANDS TO KNOW WHY YOU ISN'T OUT WATCHIN'-UP THE BIRDS THIS SPRING?
US IS A MITE CATASTROPHIED, MIZ BEAVER.
STOP PLAY-TOYIN' AROUN' AN' GIT TO WATCH-IN' BIRDS. LAW'! US'LL NOHOW GIT'EM ALL WATCHED IF YOU LALLY-GAG AN'...

BUT US IS OUTTA UNIFORM, MIZ BEAVER. US IS LOST OUR PANTS.
WHAT?! WHYN'T YOU TELL ME FIRST OFF?
YOU KNOW I ALWAYS FAINTS ON SUCH OCCASIONS. OOOOMP!

QUICK · QUICK! MIZ BEAVER, THE ROOKERY MOTHER OF THE BOY BIRD-WATCHERS IS FAINTED.

I'LL REE-VIVE HER WITH THE WATER IN THE BUCKET.

AWAKE! AWAKE --- FOR DAWN WHICH SCATTERED--- OOP!
SPLAMP!

I ADMITS I FERGOT TO REE-MOVE THEM FISH FROM THE BAIT-BUCKET BUT THAT CRAWFISH GITTIN' IN ON IT WAS HIS OWN IDEA.
FOO, A BEAUTIFUL GAL WASTES HER TIME GRACIN' UP THIS SWAMP.

US BATS ISN'T GOT A LEADER NOW WE LOST OUR PANTS. MIZ BEAVER FAINTS AN' DEACON DISAPPROVES.

'LONG AS YOU BOY BIRDWATCHERS IS HARD UP FOR A LEADER, I'LL SLIP INTO UNIFORM AN' LEAD A LI'L' FIELD TRIP.
WE ISN'T THAT HARD UP.
Albert

NOW OFF WE GO, MEN.
WE'RE OFF ALL RIGHT.
JUST WHAT I'M LOOKIN' FOR! A CHIMNEY.
HMM?
A STORK! A STORK! A SIGN OF GOOD LUCK

IF YOU IS A LUCKY STORK, WHY DOES YOU PICK ME TO NEST ON?
PLEASE TILT THE CHIMNEY UPRIGHT AN' STOP COM-PLAININ'.
OH BOY! THIS IS A LUCKY SIGN.
JUST HOLD THAT WHILST I GOES FORTH FER STICKS AN' STUFF.

WHILE HE IS PICKIN' UP TRASH I IS HIKIN' TO LAPLAND.
WHOA! YOU IS COURTIN' DEE-SASTER.

A STORK NESTIN' ON YO' CHIMNEY IS LUCKY.. BUT CHASIN' HIM OFF IS SURE DEATH.
OR WORSE
THINK IT OVER AN' KEEP YO' FLUE OPEN.

AS ROOKERY-MOTHER TO YOU BOY BIRD WATCHERS, I DE-MANDS YOU FINDS YO' PANTS AN'- SAY, WHAT AILS OL' GLOOMY-GLUM?
HE IS FALLED INTO GOOD LUCK.
LAW! LOOKS LIKE HE GOT A CASE OF THE FRITTURS... WELL, I CAN'T DO ALL TH' BIRD-GAZIN' MYSELF..

WELL, WE IS DOIN' OUR PART, WE IS WATCHIN' A BIRD RIGHT NOW.... OL' STORK!
ORK!
WHAT'S-A-MATTER WITH THE FAT OLD PARTY? SHE RUN OFF WHEN SHE SEE ME COMIN' IN WITH A LOAD OF STICKS FER THE NEST.

SO, YOU LI'L' BATS IS HELPIN' THE STORK BUILD HIS NEST IN ALBERT'S HAT?
YEP!
IT'S GOOD LUCK TO HAVE A STORK.
GOOD LUCK FOR WHO?
FER A MOMMA STORK.

D'YOU REALIZE THAT EVERY TIME THIS STORK LAYS AN EGG, YOU WILL GET BOPPED ON THE CUPOLA?
WELL ---- THEY'LL BE FRESH.

WILL IT BE POLITE FOR HIM TO LAY EGGS ON ME?
YOU CAN BET THAT IF HE DOES, HE WON'T BE NO GENTLEMAN.
OH, YOU CAN LAY TO THAT.

SO YOU LI'L' BATS IS GONNA WATCH BIRDS AT NIGHT 'CAUSE YOU IS STILL PANTS-LESS?
YEP! IT'LL BE BETTER IN THE DARK. US IS TOO EM-BARRASSED DAYTIMES.

BUT IF IT'S DARK..

HOW CAN THEY..... ??
KNOCK
BACK SO SOON? I KNEW YOU COULDN'T WATCH NOTHIN' IN THE DARK.
RIGHT! AN' NOTHIN' COULDN'T WATCH US! SO WE SWUPPED BACK OUR PANTS!
IS YOU ME OR IS I YOU? I CAN'T REMEMBER WHO WORE WHICH PANTS.
NO, I'M HIM.

DON'T LOOK SO GLUM, CHUM! NEED I REMIND YOU THAT IT'S LUCKY TO HAVE A STORK IN YOUR CHIMNEY?
YOU DON'T GOTTA REMIND ME .... YOU GOTTA CONVINCE ME.
YOU'LL BE GLAD TO KNOW THAT I HAVE A SURPRISE FOR YOU.
A SURPRISE?

TEE HEE! LOOK!
HOO BOY! THAT WILL GO GOOD WITH SAUSAGE, AN...
SIR!
DON'T LIKE SAUSAGE?

US COWBIRDS COULD USE A NEST, CONFRERE.
IS THAT THERE A NEST OR A GARBAGE CAN, COMPEER?
WELL, STILL HARBOURIN' THAT STORK, EH?
I'M TRAPPED IN FORTY FATHOM AN' CAN'T FIND THE ESCAPE HATCH.

IF I HAD THIS TO DO OVER AGAIN I WOULDN'T CONSIDER IT A-TALL.

WELL, THAT'S LIFE -- A FLEETING SHADOW, DARKSOME SEEN, AS IN A REAR-VIEW MIRROR.
IF THAT'S ADVICE YOU CAN SORT IT OUT YOUR-SELF.

LOOKS TO ME LIKE THERE'S ROOM ENOUGH IN THAT NEST FOR ALL, COMPEER COWBIRD
WITHOUT DOUBT, CONFRERE COWBIRD.
JUST BECAUSE I BUILT A STORK NEST IN YO' CHIMNEY AN' BRUNG YOU GOOD LUCK, YOU DON'T HAFTA REE-TIRE.
MMPH

I NEED A BABYSITTER. I GOTTA DO A LI'L' SHOPPIN'
AIN'T IT EARLY, MIZ STORK?

NO, IT AIN'T EARLY. SIT EASY AN' IF ANYTHIN' HATCHES GIVE ME A HOLLER.
IS YOU SURE IT'S GOOD LUCK FER ME TO HAVE MORE STORKS?

IF YOU DON'T MIND US SAYIN' SO, COMPEER, YOU IS A MIGHTY FUNNY-LOOKIN' BIRD A-SETTIN' ON THAT NEST.
SAME TO YOU, ONLY TWICE. WHAT IS YOU ANYHOWS?
US IS COWBIRDS, COMPEER...
DOVES IS WHAT! THAT IS TO SAY WE'RE DOVES, COMPEER.

IT'S GOOD YOU IS DOVES... US SWAMP FOLKS TAKES TO LI'L' DOVEY-BIRDS, BUT COWBIRDS LAYS THEY EGGS IN OTHER FOLKS' NESTS AN', WHEN THEY HATCHES, THE COW-BIRD CHILLUN THROWS THE OWNER'S CHILLUN OUT!

HOW SAD! BUT IT'S A RISKY BUSINESS TO OWN YOUR OWN NEST, COMPEER.
RISKY AN' SHAMEY, COMPEER.
DON'T BE MAD AT ME, DOVES... I'M JUST BREAKIN' THIS NEST IN FOR A FRIEND.

Boy Bird Watchers, Arise! I have sandwiches packed by yonder tree.... 'Tis time we were a-watching, fellows!
WE BEEN AT IT, PEERLESS LEADER.

WE FOUND SUCH A BIG ONE, DEAC, THAT BY WATCHIN' IT WE CAN GET ALL OUR BIRD-WATCHIN' DONE TO ONCE.

What?!? You'd watch Miz Stork? That Champion of Tradition, Emblem of Motherhood, enjoying a dignified lunch? She needs no watching!

TRUTHFULLY, WE'S JES' WATCHIN' THE LUNCH, SIR.
HAPPENS TO BE YOUR'N, SIR.
GOO?

YOU SHOULNTNA TOLD ALBERT US COWBIRDS WAS DOVES... WHOEVER HEARD OF BLACK DOVES? AN' 'SIDES I BEEN A COW-BIRD ALL MY LIFE.

UTTER DEVIATIONISM! AS A COWBIRD YOU WAS CHASED TOO! IS YOU BEEN CHASED SINCE WE BEEN DOVES? AS DOVES WE IS MESSENGERS OF PEACE AN' OUR FIRST PEACE MESSAGE IS "LAY OFF THE COWBIRDS"

PEACE AN' EQUAL RIGHTS FOR COW-BIRDS IS THE WORD FROM US UNSELFISH DOVES.
RIGHT! ROBINS GOT A RIGHT TO LAY EGGS IN NESTS WHAT ROBINS MAKE.

SO US DOVES DEFENDS THE RIGHTS OF COW-BIRDS TO LAY EGGS IN NESTS...
...WHAT ROBINS MAKES! IMPERIOUS DISCRIMINATION MUST END!! PEACE!
PEACE!

IS YOU TWO **DOVES** WILLIN' TO. TAKE A JOB **BABY-SITTIN'** FOR **MIZ STORK?**
WE DON'T BELIEVE IN MYTHOLOGICAL MATERNAL MYSTICALITY. BUT WE'LL DO IT.
COMFY?
YOUR VICTORIAN VOCABULARY IS A STIGMA-SYMBOL OF BENIGHTED PATERNALISTIC INFANTILISM.

I DUNNO **WHAT** YOU IS TALKIN' 'BOUT BUT 'LONG AS YOU KEEP THEM **EGGS** WARM **I** IS HAPPY.

WE'LL **WARM** 'EM UP **GOOD,** EH, **COMPEER**? *A POX...* *A **PROLETARIAN POX*** ON ABSENTEE LANDLORDISM.

Behold fellows, birds to watch! *What say you they are?* Dr. Moom's piebald blitherskates?
THEM IS ***LESSER*** **PIP-SQUEAKS** AN' THEY CAN WATCH THEM-SELVES
PHOO ***SOME BIRDS!***

WIPE THE **EGG** OFF YOUR MOUTH, COMPEER, THE HEAD OF AN ***AUTONOMOUS*** OUTDOOR FACTIONAL CENTER OF IDENTIFICATIONISM APPROACHES.

Well -- what might we have here?
WE'RE DOVES! FUNDAMENTALLY CONSTRUCTIVIST PRINCIPALS IN A PACIFISTIC ACTIVATION OF WORLD SCOPE ...

BY JING! YOU STEP OUTSIDE AN' SAY THAT!
HA! YOU NUGATORY NULLIFIDIAN.
RIGHT.

HA!
WHO SAY HA? WHO?
NOT ME. I IS SLEEPIN'

NAB DAG IT, MIZ STORK, YOU IS A PEEPLIN' TOM!
IS YOU THE SAME ALLIGATOR AS LAS' WEEK?

'COURSE! I IS EVEN THE SAME ONE I WAS LAST MONTH--- HAVE THE COURTESIES TO CLOSE DOWN YO' EYE LIDS!
YOU IS S'POSE TO BE BABY-SITTIN' MY EGGS.

YO' EGGS GOT LUMPY SO I QUIT.
YOU AIN'T TRUSTWORTHY
HIS
IT AIN'T ONE OF HIS FIRST-LINE VIRTUES AT THAT.

I SWEAR, MIZ STORK, YO' EGGS IS BEIN' WATCHED BY TWO DOVEY-BIRDS
YOU GOT A FLIMMERY EYE AN' A HONEY-POT TONGUE, ALBERT.
HEY, MR.TAMMANANNY, DID YOU FIND A CANDIDATE TO RUN FOR THE PRESIDENSITY?
MM

THE JOB BEEN SOUNDIN' SO TOUGH LATELY, IT LOOK LIKE NOBODY IN THE SWAMP IS SO INNOCENT AN' NAIVE AS TO BE DUPE ENOUGH TO ----

OH, I DUNNO, MR.TIGER, OUR SWAMP GOT INNOCENCE ENOUGH FOR ANY JOB.

THE CANDIDATURE

☆☆POGO☆☆ IN PERSON !!!
STUPENDOUS NEWS!
WONDROUS WORDS!
*P*O*G*O* Will RUN!!
OH, H'LO MR. BRIDGEPORT.
When I heard, I DROPPED ALL!
The CIRCUS SEASON WEEPS ITS INFANT PLEADING to NO AVAIL!
{Let me carry that for YOU, candidate.}
3 (three) COUNT THEM (three) 3 CHEERS!

I, P.T. BRIDGEPORT, at GREAT personal EXPENSE and SACRIFICE will guide your EVERY STEP!
I SAID TO REGINALD HERE, "BREWSTER, DEAR CHAP," I SAID, "I....
BOLINGBROKE, my boy, at least have the decency to cease that ☆IN-FERN-AL☆ drumming when I'm talking about YOU! THERE'S A GOOD LAD, HEWLITT!
I GOTTA GIT MY DRUMMIN' DONE, Y'KNOW.

DON'T FORGET, POGO, MY BOY, I stand ready to direct YOU FULLY IN YOUR CAMPAIGN!
DOGGONE, MR. BRIDGEPORT, I ISN'T SAID I'D RUN!
This is SERIOUS! you should feel it's an HONOR TO SERVE YOUR FRIENDS ☆☆

Rest assured, Pogo, dear lad, your friends RETURN THE Feeling!! It is !! RE-CIP-RO-CAL!!
WHATS YOU MEAN? THEY'D BE HONORED TO SERVE ME?
HOW'S THAT, SON?
NO, HE MEANS THEY'D GO 'LONG WITH YOU ---- THEY'D AGREE IT WAS A HONOR FOR YOU TO SERVE YOUR FRIENDS.

WE DOVES ARE A HARD CORE PACIFIC GROUP IN AMICABLE OCCUPATIONAL DUTY BOUND TO THE BASIC TENETS OF MATERNO-DOMICILICAL FUNCTION.
"Must be Doves! Did you ever hear such high-tone talk?
AN' SO BRAINY AN' INCOMPREHENSIBOBBLE
"Behold, Pogo! Doves have nested! What a Happy Omen for your candidature
IS I?

THESE DOVES LOOKS LIKE COWBIRDS; SOUNDS LIKE COWBIRDS AN' IS SETTIN' IN SOMEBODY ELSE'S NEST ON COWBIRD EGGS JUST LIKE COWBIRDS.
TARNATION! THE CANDIDATE KNOWS EVER'THIN'. HE KIN COUNTER-DICT US BIRD EXPERTS ... HE KIN INSULT THE MATERNO-DOMICKOWICKAL FUNCTION LIKE WHAT THE DOVES SAY ... WHAT ELSE DO HE KNOW?
I KNOWS THE BEST BIRD BRAINS IN THE COUNTRY IS A-GIN ME.

Do you chaps realize that Pogo has lashed out at "Motherhood and Peace? He says the doves what is baby-sittin' for Miz Stork is Cowbirds!"
IT'S THE WATER

WE TOOK THAT UP WITH THEM CHIMNEY-COLORED DOVES TOO... SHOWED 'EM COWBIRD PICTURES IN THE BIRD BOOK LOOKED LIKE 'EM... THEY SAID: "DON'T GIVE IT A DEVIATIONAL THOUGHT."
IT'S THE WATER

They are above such non-sense, I'll wager a pretty--
BLESS THEIR HEARTS.

YEP! THEY IS ABOVE AN' BEE-YOND! THEY TOOK THE OLD BOOK AN' SET FIRE TO IT... NOW THEY IS WRITIN' A BRANG NEW ONE..... SOMETHIN' TO CONFORM TO THE FACTS.
HARD A-LEE HARD A-PORT AN HARD AVAST.
IT'S THE WATER

AS ROOKERY-MOTHER TO THE BOY BIRD WATCHERS I IS BEEN BUSY HELPIN' THE DEACON PROTECT THE DOVES WHAT BEEN GUARDIN' YOUR NEST...
I'M EVER SO GRATEFUL TO YOU GIRLS.
Mmmp
POGO BEEN SPREADIN' PURE POISON 'BOUT HOW YOU IS HARBOURIN' COWBIRDS!
MY LAND! I NEVER DID!
Scandalous

THERE THEY IS, MOTHER STORK...
YEEP! THEM DOVES IS COWBIRDS!
AN INFORMER! A QUEASY CLASS-RIDDEN INHIBITIONIST!
PSSST... DON'T THROW THAT-- IT'S ONE OF OURS.

AHA! I see they are chasing the COWBIRDS!
WHEN THEY ASKED ME I TOLE 'EM AN' I TOLE 'EM--- "THEY ISN'T DOVES!" I TOLE 'EM.
As a candidate. you should answer controversial Questions with "No Comment"
BUT I HAD COMMENT SO I GUV IT.

you must word answers so that you don't 'SPOIL' the Questions.
BUT THE PUBLIC WANTS TO KNOW WHERE A MAN STANDS!
THEN HE SHOULD SAY: "DUE to incalculable potentials apparently inherent pro and con in aspects of the to-be determinationism of current trends I regret that..
ANYBODY LEFT LISTENIN' WOULD OF STOPPED BY THAT TIME.

HOT DOG! NOW THEM COWBIRDS IS GONE, I CAN GIT MY HAT BACK AN' EMPTY THAT RATTY NEST OUTEN IT.

Desist ... begone! Unhand that Symbol of Mother and Fireside! We Bird Watchers will not allow Miz Stork's home to again be despoiled.

MIZ STORK BUILT THAT NEST IN MY HAT FOR WHICH SHE HAD NO MORE OF A RIGHT TO DO IT THAN THEM COWBIRDS HAD TO TAKE IT OVER OFF'N HER WITHOUT SHE SAY SO AND I...
You'll touch this..

..over my dead body.
I'SE WILLIN' ..... ANY WAY YOU SAY. STAY THERE WHILST I GITS A FLYSWATTER.

HEY, POGO! THE TALK IN THE SALONS AROUND FORT MUDGE IS THAT YOUR HAT'S IN THE RING.
DON'T MENTION HATS, MOUSE.
YEAH! OL' DEACON IS GUV MY HAT TO MIZ STORK WITH-OUT SO MUCH AS A BAYOU-LEAVE.
THE S.S. GENERAL

WHAT IN THE WORLD DOES SHE WANT WITH YOUR HAT?
SHE BUILT A NEST IN IT.

ABANDON IT THEN.... ONCE A PARTY IS NESTED, NEVER DISTURB IT... I MIND ONE TIME ME AN' LUCKY JACK LARKIN BUILT US A NEST OF SCRAPS IN THE DERBY OF A EMINENT BANK PRES. ... WELL, SIR... WE JUST GOT..
A FAVORABLE GAME GOIN' WHEN THE PREXY GRABS HIS LID AN' GOES TO LUNCH. WE WAS ALL HAULED IN FOR ABSCONDIMENT... SEEMS WE'D TORE UP LARGE BILLS FOR THE NEST .. THE PRES. WAS A GOOD MAN TO BE IN THE POKEY WITH .. HE ..
HEY!

TAMMANANNY, A GROSS BLOW has befallen POGO'S CANDIDATURE
HE'S MADE A SPEECH?

NO, he was mixed up with some COWBIRDS! The Deacon claims it blackens POGO'S name
SOMEONE MUST ENDORSE POGO'S CHARACTER!

YES! It will take a man of PROVEN MERIT! A CITIZEN WHO TOWERS ABOVE THE CROWD. ★★ A FIGURE ADMIRED and BELOVED by ALL!!!
IT'LL BE HARD TO GET SUCH A MAN TO SPEAK UP AND RISK HIS OWN GOOD NAME.
SAY NOT SO!! These are TIMES for STALWARCY & PLUCK One noble soul must risk it I, P.T. BRIDGEPORT WILL SPEAK FOR POGO!!
YOU SURE THAT FIGURE IS UNIVERSALLY ADMIRED?

WE SEE MR. P.T. BRIDGEPORT STRIDIN' MAN-FUL OFF.... WHAT'S UP?
DEACON'S BEEN SMIRCHIN' UP OL' POGO'S NAME ... SO P.T. IS GONNA TELL 'EM A MOUTHFUL.

FRIENDS, I am here to

THEM COWBIRDS LEFT THEIR OWN EGGS IN MY NEST.

S'MATTER, SWALLOW YOUR TONGUE?
not My Tongue, NO!
HMMPH... SOME MOUTHFUL.
I NEVER DID HOLD WITH BEARS

WELL, I GUESS WE WON'T BE VOTIN' FOR POGO!
GONNA WRITE IN YOUR OWN SELFS?

'COURSE NOT! IT WOULDN'T BE FAIR TO PRECIPITATE A LAND-SLIDE. BUT POGO'S CAMPAIGN MANAGER IS HAD IT PROVED TO HIM THAT THERE'S A GROUND SWELL OF OPINION AGAINST POGO.
HOW PROVED?

HE GOT UP TO SPEAK FOR THE CANDIDATE AN' GOT THROWN AT WITH EGGS' THAT SHOWS POGO IS WASHED UP. THE PUBLIC IS SPOKE! FAIR MINDED AN' SQUARE ...UH-M-
.. HEADED?

WELL, BULLY FOR YOU, BOYS. KEEP FINGERIN' THE PULSE OF THE GRASS ROOTS ... BUT TRY TO HOLD OFF WRITIN' IN YOUR OWN NAMES. IT'LL BE TOUGH BECAUSE CONSTANT PROOF OF OTHER CANDIDATES' CRIMINAL WAYS WILL ARISE...
US'LL BE FIRM AN' REFRAIN 'CAUSE IT WOULDN'T BE SPORTIN'...
THRU ELECTION DAY?

YOU CAN STOP MAKIN' THEM MACHINE VOTERS.... IT'S TIME WE WAS ALL BEIN' GOOD FRIENDS WITH P.T. BRIDGEPORT.
WHAT ?
U.S. MAIL

WHY, THAT BIG OL' BLOWHEAD! HE'S A REAL FIRST OF MAY CIRCUS CIPHER ... A RUBE IN DISGUISE ... A SAWDUST FOGHORN... WHAT'S HE GOT TO BE FRIENDS WITH?
M M

A BIG BAG OF MONEY.
LEMME HELP YOU CARRY THAT TO THE DEAR DEAR OLD PARTY! WHO'S SENDIN' THIS DIRTY OLD MONEY TO THE SWEET EVER-LOVIN' CHAP? HE'S GONE NEED A HAND COUNTIN' IT.
STOP SHOVIN'. AIN'T NO SPECIAL DEE-LIVERY STAMP ON IT.

LET'S JES' LOOK AT THE MONEY WHAT BEEN SENT TO P.T. BRIDGEPORT... HE WON'T MISS A LI'L BIT IF WE.. HEEHOOHAHA
STOP THAT! THIS MAIL MIGHT BE FOURTH CLASS BUT...
THE BAG COULD OF BEEN DAMAGED IN TRANSIT.
HEEHEEHO HOHOOHA HAHOHEE!
I HAD A FRIEND TRIED THAT ONCE AN' HE WOUND UP IN THE BIG ARENA PLAYIN' A 20 YEAR GAME OF ROCK HOCKEY.

20 YEARS ?
THE KIND OF GIDDY FRIENDS YOU HAVE, PROB'LY NEED LESSONS LIKE THAT.... CHUG-CHUG, STOP HOLDIN' US UP! GIT GOIN' FOR P.T. BRIDGEPORT'S PLACE.
HOLD UP! IT'S AGIN REGULATIONS TO RUSH FOURTH CLASS MAIL.

DON'T FERGIT TO REMIND P.T. NOW, THAT THIS BAG OF MONEY WAS HEAVY AN' HE COULD SHOW HIS APPRECIATION BY.. HEEHO HAHONEEHAHEE
U.S AND A MAIL
WE WAS WONDERIN', MR. BRIDGEPORT, (SEEIN' AS WE BRUNG THAT BAGFUL) IF WE COULD DIP IN AN.. AW HAW
HEE HOO HAHA HA
A REASONABLE REQUEST, Take all you wish!
WOW, ALL?

of COURSE, OWL! HELP YOUR'SELF TO BUTTONS!
BUTTONS ?

AYE --- aren't they BEAUTIES? POGO BUTTONS for --- his CANDIDATURE ------- ------- EMBLAZONED = I GO POGO!

EVERYBODY in the Swamp IS GOING FOR POGO for PRESIDENT!!! EVERYBODY ★ EVERYBODY
EV-AR-EE-BOD-DEE --

'CEPT POGO.

DID YOU SEE THE BUTTONS THAT OL' P.T. BRIDGEPORT IS GIVIN' OUT?
"Mmm-Campaign buttons-For Pogo? What you wearin' em for?

THEY WAS FREE.
GO POGO

There must be some way that we dignified few opposed to "P.T. Bridgeport's gang can make use of these buttons.....
I MADE USE OF MINE!
A BUTTON COMED OFF'N MY UNDERWEARS BUT I HOLTS 'EM UP WITH MY GOOD OL' POGO BADGE ... GOTTA GIT HOME 'CAUSE IT'S LUMPY.
SEE, A WHOLE FOLK SENTIMENT IS BEIN' BUILT UP.

YOU WIN THAT ONE.
Gentlemen, a few dignified citizens would let bygones be gone if Pogo would be OUR candidate.
THAT'S ONE EACH THEN.
SHH.. WE IS SEEIN' WHO KIN DREAM 'BOUT TH' BIGGEST CAT-FISH.
We oppose the "P.T. Bridgeport gang.- If Pogo would come out on the side of Right -- i.e. OUR side --- Fighting--

YOU'D FERGIT POGO WAS "MIXED UP WITH COWBIRDS"? DEACON, DID YOU EVER SEE TWO DOGS FIGHTIN' OVER A BONE?
Naturally

---YOU EVER SEE THE BONE FIGHT?

RIGHT ON THE BUTTON

yes, Gunther, YES!! NOW LISTEN To the SPEECH
WHILE YOU'RE DOIN' THAT, I'LL PRACTICE MY NEW CONCESSION.
PEANUTS!
Fearless
HONESTY
VOTER
Loyalty

GREAT NEWS, POGO!! CHURCHY has written a SONG for your CAMPAIGN!
IS I GOT A CAMPAIGN?

OH, ONCE THE OPPOSITION WAS COMPLETALLY OPPOSED TO ALL THE SUPPOSITIONS THAT WAS GEN'RALLY SUPPOSED; AN' NOW THE SUPERSTITIONS THAT WERE THO'T TO BE IMPOSED ARE SEEN BY COMPOSITION TO BE SLIGHTLY DECOMPOSED!
THERE !!!!

It's a BANNER of BRAVERY ~~ a FLAG OF FREEDOM FLUNG TO THE WINDS of HEAVEN ~~~~ A TRUMPET OF TRIUMPH wafting a veritable vibrato-bravura of words writ in tears meaning ~uh m~~ uh ~~ mm-meaning ~~
GO POGO

What does it mean, Turtle?
WHAT?
STOP BUNKO

FRIENDS! I WELCOME Each and Every ONE to this Monster Rally!!
STOP BUNKO
SO FAR, ONLY ONE MONSTER.
I GIVE YOU Brother OWL, who has a FEW WORDS to say on behalf of the CANDIDATE
ANOTHER ONE
AN', BY JING, THEY AIN'T GIVIN' THAT ONE TO ME!

A little less impulsive Shoving, friend, WOULD-
I THOUGHT YOU HAD A BROADER PLATFORM!
THE MONSTERS ARE RALLYING.

It might be of interest for
you to become AWARE,
that this UNSEEMLY
REFLECTS NO CREDIT ON THE
ISSUES OF
IF YOU WOULD CLOSE THAT BIG BAZOO AND LET ME
PEANUTS!
APTLY WORDED!
THERE'S AS EARY A MONSTER AS ANY PARTY EVER SPAWNED.

YOU INVITED ME TO THE ROSTRUM TO MAKE A SPEECH AND BY WILLY DINGO I'M A-GONNA MAKE IT.
SIR, don't be so CROWDY!
STOP BUNKO
I'M HERE WITH A NEW CAMPAIGN SONG.

A PLATFORM OUGHTA BE BIG ENUFF FER TH' WHOLE PARTY.
This AIN'T NO PARTY! IT'S a unruly RALLY REALLY!
AHEM!

I'M PUTTIN' MY FOOT DOWN!
THERE'S ONE NAME TONIGHT, ONE STAR THAT SPANGLES BRIGHT, ONE HEART WHOSE STRIPE IS WHITE AND WIDELY RED AND RIGHT.....
BOOM
IT'S
PEANUTS!
PEANUTS!
PEANUTS
FOR ALL!

COUSIN COWBIRD, MINE COMPEER, WE'VE BEEN HARRIED AND HUNTED TOO LONG!
RIGHT! IT IS TIME WE FIGHTERS FOR THE GOOD LIFE REVEALED THE POWER OF OUR HAND.

LET US THROW UP A BARRICADE AGAINST THE GRINDING HEELS OF EXPLOITATION!
AYE! WE'LL BE HEROES IN THE RANKS, SOLDIERS FOR EQUALITY!

WILL WE TURN TAIL LIKE COWARDLY DOGS OF PROPERTY?
NO!
WILL WE BEG FOR ALMS?
NO!
WHAT WILL WE DO? CRAWL?
NO!
WILL WE BE STRONG IN THE MIGHT OF OUR RIGHT?
YES! YES! WE'LL HIDE IN HERE.

SO! THIS IS THE HOME OF POGO~ PALATIAL AND GROSS IN ITS MERCENARY MUNDANITY!
STUFFED WITH THE FRUIT OF OUR NATURAL RESOURCES ALL EXCISED FROM THE PUBLIC ESTATE!

BLED FROM STORES WITH MONEY EARNED UNDER A DECADENT CASH AN' CARRY SYSTEM
HE THRIVES ONLY UNDER THE THRALLDOM OF THRIFT! A SHIFTY DEVICE!
COOKIE

AND HOW DOES HE PROTECT THESE RIGHTFUL TREASURES OF WE HARASSED HORDES? HE LEAVES HIS DOOR OPEN!
BENIGHTED FRATERNALISM! A CLEAR CASE.

YES, A SUBVERSION OF THE BASIC TENETS OF PUBLIC PROPERTY PRIVACY.
IRRESPONSIBILISM! HE ACTS AS IF HE DIDN'T CARE WHO WANDERED IN HERE.

DON'T SEEM LIKE POGO IS HOME, SO I'LL LEAVE THESE "I GO POGO" BADGES OUT HERE.
POGO

HMMPH! POGO'S HAD ANOTHER DELIVERY OF GROCERIES.
AND ABOUT TIME... LOOKS LIKE A FLIMSY BOURGEOIS BAG OF BEANS.

POUR ON POGO'S KETCHUP HEAVY... I LIKES 'EM TASTEFUL!

OW! THESE AIN'T BEANS! THEY'RE CAMPAIGN PINS!
THAT SNEAKY POGO! MISREPRESENTIN' THESE AS BEANS.

YOO HOO!
YOWP! WHAT'S YOU?

'LONG AS YOU IS RUNNIN' FOR PRESIDENT, I IS GONE BE YO' MILITARY AIDE. US WILL BOWL OVER THE OPPOSITION.

LIKE SO!
BRAM

I DUNNO... SEEM LIKE MILITARY AIDES IS MORE SHOT AT THAN BY.

AS YO' MILITARY AIDE, POGO, I OUGHTA LOOK AT YO' CABINET AN' SEE WHO GONE BE IN IT.

WE IS!
YEOW.
COW BIRDS!

MY SAKES! HOW'S YOU GONE GIT YO' LEG OUT?
I GOT A IDEA!
IT'S STUCK.

I'LL JUST PULL THE CORD AN' THE CHARGE WILL BLOW THE ....
STOP! DO YOU WANTA DEEFEN US ALL BY FIRIN' THAT THING INDOORS?

'LONG AS WE IS CONFINED HERE WHILST YOU IS STUCK IN THE CANNON, ME AN' MY COUSIN COWBIRD WILL DO ALL THE COOKIN'....
UNTIL SOME-BODY COM-PLAINS 'BOUT THE FOOD--- THEN HE GOTTA COOK.

WE'LL GIT HIM TO COMPLAIN EARLY. WE'LL SERVE HIM THE "I GO POGO" BUTTONS WE COOKED UP, THINKIN' THEY WAS BEANS.

AAKK!
THIS BLAGSTAG, DOGBONED, FOGBOUND GOOK TASTES LIKE RUSTY OL' CAMPAIGN BUTTONS.

GOOD, THOUGH!

DON'T LIKE HAVIN' THEM COWBIRDS STAYIN' HERE. I DEE-SPISES 'EM FOR ALLUS SPONGIN' OFF OTHERS .... BUT SOUTHERN HOSPITALITY RULES.
THEY'S WORSE TROUBLES .... YO' FOOT BEIN' STUCK IN A CANNON FR INSTINCT.

GUESS WE CAN SNEAK IN AN' BORRY SUGAR NOW ... THEY'S SLEEPIN'

I KEEPS TRACK OF ALL I BORROWS ... ... I OWES POGO 17,615 POUNDS NOW.... 'TAINT LIKE I WAS CHEATIN' HIM OUTEN IT.
MY DREAMS ARE BAD ENOUGH ... GO AWAY.

It was all I could do to spoon the sugar out over them no-good cowbirds! Imagine the Candidate having such Mountebankery in his Cabinet!!
DISGUSTIN'! IF ANYBODY ELSE HAD SUGAR, I WOULDN'T TAKE OFF'N POGO.
POGO

COULD MEBBE YOU FOTCH ME A COOKIE AN' A GLASS OF MILK SEEIN' AS I IS YO' MILITARY AIDE, PRES. ?
I ISN'T BEEN ELECTED TO TH' PRESIDENSITY YET.....

SORRY, POGO! US COWBIRDS GOT HERE FIRST AN' YO' COOKIES BAD AS THEY IS ... IS GONE.
COOKIES

ALBERT'S GONE HAFTA SETTLE FOR A GLASS OF MILK.

GIT A-WAY! DOESN'T YOU RESPECK THE BATHIN' PRIVACY OF A HOUSE GUEST?
MILK

YOU FIGGER IF I GITS ELECTED TO SOMETHIN' I KIN MAKE HOSPITALITY A FEDERABLE O-FFENSE ?

I see you're wearing an "I GO POGO" button, Porky.
I SEE YOU IS, TOO.

Not out of choice, my good fellow. It's the only pin here, my dear chap.
EVEN THO' IT'S CROOKED, IT'S THE ONE WHEEL IN TOWN, HUH? AN' I'M NOT NO-BODY'S CHAP.... DEAR OR OTHER.

Eh? Do you know this Pogo has COWBIRDS in his cabinet? Strange bedfellows, I must say.......
POGO SLEEPIN' IN HIS OWN CUPBOARD? WELL, YOU BEEN INTO IT ENOUGH; BORRY-FYIN' AN' ALL.
WHAT'S THE DIFFERMINTS IF THEM OUT-LANDERS EAT POGO OUTEN HOUSE AN' HOME OR YOU DOES ?
Why, I'm a Friend of Pogo! Where's your sense of commun-ity Spirit?

FOLKS KEEP ASKIN' WHAT YOU STANDS FOR WHEN YOU STANDS FOR COWBIRDS.
NOT MUCH LONGER-- I IS GONE DO SOME-THIN'....
POGO SAY HE GONE SET FIRE TO HIS HOUSE.
NOT WHILST HE GIVIN' US HAVEN HE CAN'T---- WE IS ILL!

SO IS I ... MOOM OVER!

IF YOU'LL FORGIVE ME FER SAYIN' SO, PORKYPINES GOT THEIR POINTS.
YEP, IF I WARN'T A-TTACHED TO MYSELF, I WOULDN'T SLEEP WITH ME EITHER.

LEFT AT THE POST

HERE, borrow mine and remember ☞ Throwing ONE'S HAT INTO THE RING REQUIRES ☆☆ STANCE ☆☆ and STAMINA
6-17

STANCE AN' STAMINA PLAYED THE OLD PALACE WITH ME IN---
PROPERTY DEPT.

BAM!
--19-OUGHT-22.
DIST. BY POST-HALL SYNDICATE.

THEY DON'T MAKE THESE BOATERS LIKE THEY USE TO.
YOU LOAD THAT FOWLING PIECE WITH COLD OATMEAL from now on--- I might of been IN THAT!
COPR 1952 WALT KELLY

AND THEN :

GOT ANY OL' PLANK? THE CRITTURS IS A-BUILDERIN' YOU A PLATFORM--- LEAST US KIN DO IS COUNTERBUTE.
6-23
DIST. BY POST-HALL SYNDICATE.

PIECE OF MY PORCH DO?
SURE, THEY WAS A PORCH PLANK IN THE LAST PLATFORM.
POGO

WHOA! BACK OFF!
YEAH! YOU'RE A LI'L' LATE. US ALL GOT HERE FIRST WITH OUR PLANKS...NO MORE ROOM!
WE MERE WAS TRYIN' TO HELP.

SORRY, MR. CANDIDATE.
WELL, THEY IS NICE TO GO TO SO MUCH FUSS. AN' I WOULDN'T WANT TO BE CROWDY.
COPR. 1962 WALT KELLY

WHAT'S THEY UP TO, COMPEER?
EMPLOYING A FUNCTIONAL OBSCURATION OF POLITICAL EXTRINSICALISM..NAMELY, BUILDIN' A PLATFORM.
6-24
DIST. BY POST-HALL SYNDICATE

WITHOUT BEING SUCKED INTO THE MAELSTROM OF JUVENILE FOLKWAYS.... IT WOULD AID OUR PEACEFUL AIMS OF WORLDWIDE PARTICIPATORY PROGRESS IF WE HAD A PLATFORM.
TOOK THE WORDS RIGHT OUT OF MY BIG MOUTH.

WE COULD JOIN THEIR MUDDY MINDED MELANGENOUS MEE-NAGERY AND THEN FORM A SPLINTER PARTY...
WHEE...
COPR. 1962 WALT KELLY

PER-RISH THE THOUGHT, COMPEER.

ME AN' BEMILDRED IS GONE LAUNCH POGO'S PLATFORM BY CRACKIN' A BOTTLE OF GHASTLY WATER ON ITS BROW.
6-25 DIST. BY POST-HALL SYNDICATE
GOOD, 'CAUSE I IS READIED-UP A CAMPAIGN SONG CALLED "THE THIRD RAIL THEME."
"The Party of the first Part
And the party of the next
Are partly participled
In a parsley-covered text..."

"Were you partial to a Party
That has parceled out its parts
With the Party that was second
In your polly-tickle heart?
"Then parlay all your losings
On a horse that's running dark...
With lights-out you may triple
In a homer in the park."
HEY, YOU DON'T LAUNCH A PLATFORM THAT WAY.
I KNOW... I MISSED HIM.
COPR. 1962 WALT KELLY

AND THEN:
SO, YOU IS MAKIN' SAN'WICHES FOR THE TRIP TO CHICAGO?
YEP! OL' ALBERT GITS HONGRIFIED!
6-30

'TIL HE GOT MAD AN' KICKED THE CANNON TO PIECES WHAT WERE STUCK ON HIS FOOT, IT DIN'T LOOK LIKE HE'D GO.
GOTTA FIND OWL. HE'S IN CHARGE OF THE A-RRANGE MINTS.

GOT A LI'L' SOMETHIN FOR YOU TO.....
PUL-LEASE, MISTER CANDIDATE! NO MORE FAVORS FOR NO-BODY... I IS A BUSY MAN--- WHATEVER YOU GOT, FOR-GET IT.
IF YOU'LL LISTEN TO MY CAMPAIGN SONGS, I'LL HELP YOU EAT THEM SAN'WICHES.....
YOU IS DECENT, CHURCHY.
DIST. BY POST-HALL SYNDICATE
COPR 1952 WALT KELLY

POGO! WE CAME TO SEE THE PLAT-FORM THEY MADE FOR YOU.
SHH... TURTLE IS GONE SING SOME MORE OF THE CAMPAIGN SONG HE WROT, "THE THIRD RAIL THEME."
"Promulge the prating prim
Of the prudent PromiSOR,
For the Premise of the Promise
Was the PrimogenitOR
Of the Primalaceous Program
With the Presbyopic DOOR!"
LUNCH
7-1

IT'S ALMOST UNPOSSIBOBBLE TO EAT AND REE-CITE AT THE SAME TIME.
THAT IS ALL-READY OCCURRED TO US.
NOTE IT has ★★WET★PLANKS And DRY!
EXCELLENT, P.T., EX-CELL-LENT!
LUNCH
DIST BY POST-HALL SYNDICATE

YOU FOLKS GOT TIME TO SEE WHAT I GOT **RINGED** UP FOR **CHICAGO** SO'S US KIN NOMINATE OUR ***CANDIDATE?***
THESE TWO IS BUSY WRITIN' POLITICAL PROM-ISES WITH BOTH HANDS... ***WHAT'S*** YOU **GOT?**
6-27
DIST. BY POST-HALL SYNDICATE

I'LL PULL IT OVER SO'S YOU CAN SEE .... ***IT'S A PORTABLE***...

---**SMOKE-FILLED** ROOM! I STOKES THE STOVE WITH OL' **SEE**-*GAR* BUTTS AN'...
SHOO-BOY! A MAN COULD SMOKE A ***HOG*** IN A LI'L ROOM LIKE THAT.
I DUNNO--- SOME OF THEM CANDIDATES DON'T CURE EASY.
COPR. 1952 WALT KELLY

MY PORTABLE SMOKE-FILLED ROOM IS BOUND TO GIT YO' CANDIDATE **NOM**INATED.
EVERYBODY *WHO* IS *Anybody* IS GOING.
EVEN **SOME** WHO ISN'T.
IS CHICAGO IN **INDIANA** OR ***MASSACHUSETTS***?
OHIO.
MOE, AS I LIVE AN' **BREATHE**.... HOW'S THE MOTHIN' GAME?
BAD--I FOLLOWS THE WORD; LAYS EGGS ON **CROWS**; THE CATERPIGGLES HATCH OUT AN' GIT SHOOK OFF. *I'M GOIN' INTO AN-OTHER* ***LINE***.
7-3
DIST BY POST-HALL SYNDICATE.

YOU LOCKS ALL THE POLITICIANS INSIDE AND TURN ON THE SMOKE.
I'M FOR BI-PARTISAN FOREIGN RELATIONS.
YOU USE CROWS?
CROWS.
AN' WHEN YOU MENTIONS YO' MAN---?
THEY IS IN TEARS
A FOREIGN RELATION OF MINE WENT WITH ALL THE PARTIES ONE YEAR. NAME OF MABEL.
WAY I HEERD, IT'S CLOTHES YOU USE.
OH, CLOTHES? I'LL GIVE 'EM A TRY.
COPR 1952 WALT KELLY

BOY! OFF TO CHICAGO AT LAST--- WAIT'LL WE UNVEIL OUR CANDIDATE, MISTER, POGO POSSUM.. HA!
WOW! I GO POGO!
OWL! I GOT A FEELIN' WE IS LEFT SOME-THIN' BE-HIND.
HOO BOY!
HEAR! HEAR!!
THE CRIMSON
7-4

CAN'T THINK OF NOTHIN'.... LESSEN IT'S A SACK OF I GO POGO PINS.
AN' WE WOULDN'T GO WITHOUT ALL OUR BUTTONS.
NO GO?
ZZ ZZ
BUTTONS
COPR. 1952 WALT KELLY.
DIST. BY POST-HALL SYNDICATE

FREE TO GET READY and SORE TO GO

WHY SO IT IS! A COWBIRD.... HE LOOKS A LITTLE PEAKIED.
WELL, THROW IT AWAY THEN... THEY COMMON ENOUGH.
DISGUSTING SO! THERE'S ONE.

AARGH HE DEVIATED.
ORDERS
I'LL SET YOU DOWN CAREFUL.... OW
YOU CAPITALIST! WEARIN' A HAT.

HA! YOU'VE GOT ONE ON YOU.
I HAVE NOT.
YOU HAVE TOO!
I HAVE NOT!

OH, I SHALL SMITE YOU TO A SMITHEREEN!

BY THOR! YOU WILL GET A NASTY LETTER FROM MY LAWYER IN THE MORNING.

THIS WILL ONLY LEAD TO BLOWS, I WARN YOU.

LOOK! LOOK! ONE OF THEM THERE IS GETTIN' AWAY!
LOOK! LOOK! ONE OF THEM THERE IS GETTIN' A WAY.

SHEER ME-TOO ISM! WHY DON'T YOU USE YOUR OWN HEAD.?
YOURS IS GOT BIG ENOUGH FOR BOTH OF US.

ONE OF WHAT WHERE IS GETTIN' AWAY?
ONE OF THE GINGER-BREAD BOYS IS RUN OFF. WE MUST GIVE CHASE.

YOU CAN RUN AN' RUN AS FATS AS YOU CAN -- BUT YOU CAN'T CATCH ME, I'M A GINGER-BREAD MAN.
COME BACK, YOU TRAITOR .... COME BACK
MIGHT AS WELL USE THE SAME BALLOONS.
WHOO! I'M A LI'L' WINDED.
GLAD TO MEET YOU! I'M A LI'L' ELEPHANT.
THERE'S NO SUCH THINGAS A LITTLE ELEPHANT.
WHY WAS THAT GINGERBREAD BOY RUNNIN' OFF?
HE WAS DESERTIN'
WE WAS GOIN' TO SHIP HIM TO THE ARMY OF THE REALM --- BUT HE QUIT --- IT MAKES ME MAD.
ME TOO
THE ARMY OF THE WHOM? THEY LIKES GINGERBREAD BOYS?
THEY ARE GINGERBREAD BOYS ... NOW COWBIRDS WILL GET THIS ONE.

AND THEY, LIKE AS NOT, WILL CONVERT HIM.
CONVERT HIM?
YES, INTO FOOD.
BUT WE MUST NOT DWELL ON GINGERBREAD BOYS WHO'D SOLDIERS BE.
OUT OF SIGHT ... OUT OF MIND.

THEY'RE OUT OF SIGHT ... WE'RE OUT OF MIND? WHY NOT SAVE THE GINGERBREAD BOY?
BECAUSE WE ARE BUSY PLAYIN' NATIONAL PASTIMES ... HIGH-LOW TARIFF AN' THE GAME ...
AN' NEXT WE IS GONE PLAY AT JACKSTRAWS. MEBBE I'LL GIT TO WIN.

PIG! YOU WON TWENTY-FOUR YEARS AGO.
NOT SO'S IT REALLY COUNTED, REALLY.
SAY!
YOU THERE! HOW'D YOU LIKE TO PLAY?
PLAY WHAT?

GINGER BREAD BOY!
GIVE US A TASTE.
SHAKE HIM UP! IT'LL GET THE FLAVOR ROUSED.
SHAKE HIM UP.. WAKE HIM UP...
WAKE UP, UNCLE POGO! WAKE UP!
GOSH.... RACKETY-COON CHILE, I MUST OF WAS DREAMIN'.
ISN'T YOU GONE GO AN' GIT ELECTED PRESIDENT?
WELL, I DUNNO...I'LL GO 'LONG AN' VOTE FOR EVERYBODY IN SIGHT... THAT WAY WE'LL GIT A GOOD ONE... Y'KNOW, CHILE, CRITTERS IS NICE, BUT HUMAN BEANS STILL MAKES THE BEST PEOPLE.
NOW, YOU GOT NO CALL TO BE TALKIN' CRANKY JES' 'CAUSE YOU IS FRESH WOKE.